KANT

ČESKÉ DOMY

CZECH HOUSES

Ján Stempel
Jan Jakub Tesař
Ondřej Beneš

KANT

CZECH HOUSES

Autors | Ján Stempel, Jan Jakub Tesař, Ondřej Beneš
Peer Reviews | Eugene Asse, Ákos Moravánszky, Adam Gebrian
Translation | Vladimír Mašinský, Stephan von Pohl
Proofreading | Stephan von Pohl
Design and typesetting | Karel Kerlický
Prepress | KANT
Printed in the Czech Republic by PB tisk Příbram
Published by KANT – Karel Kerlický, 2014
kant@kant-books.com
ISBN 978-80-7437-140-0

All layouts of houses are in the same scale of 1:333

CONTENT

Authors:

Ján Stempel

Architect, Professor at the Faculty of Architecture, Czech Technical University in Prague

Jan Jakub Tesař

Architect, Assistant professor at the Faculty of Architecture, Czech Technical University in Prague

Ondřej Beneš

Architect, Assistant professor at the Faculty of Architecture, Czech Technical University in Prague

Introduction

In the fields of architecture and urbanism, *individual housing* such as single-family homes, villas, luxury residences, recreational objects, or farmsteads represents an important segment. The quality and manner of implementation of this, one of the oldest architectural forms, can be used to infer the "state of society". Housing represents one of mankind's basic needs; though it is something that we may take for granted at first glance, it is a part of cultural changes and civilizational development, including the possibilities opened up by new construction technologies.

Between the wars, architecture in Czechoslovakia was an integral part of the most progressive developments in the field, and outstanding projects such as the Villa Tugendhat by Mies van der Rohe in Brno and Adolf Loos's Müller Villa in Prague are recognized as pinnacle achievements of world architecture. After 1948, these international ties suffered as the country's leaders dictated "Socialist Realism" from above. The Brussels pavilion (1958) and the return to "authentic architecture" paved the way for the realization of exceptional projects in the 1960s, including a surge in the construction of single-family homes.

However, over the subsequent decades (in particular the normalization-era 1970s and '80s) the lack of state support for individual housing stifled the sector's promising future. Personal self-realization, which was often limited at work, found an expression in the construction of family homes built by the owners themselves – which in this context represented a form of "internal emigration".

A fundamental change comes with the year 1989, which marks the end of central planning, inefficient production, heavy industry, and suppressed individual housing construction. The new market economy brings with it a "society of mass consumption" and a civic and democratic society, accompanied by an increase in individualism. With the privatization of the 1990s, the abrupt transformation of ownership relations leads to the creation of a new sociology within society, which is reflected in the architect's relationship to the client and gives rise to a new intermediary, the developer.

By this we mean to say: "large and small" changes in society, as well as the seismic societal since 1989 (including changes in consumption and people's interests and aspirations) have become permanently inscribed within the unique segment of *family homes. In fact, during this era the segment of family homes, villas, and luxury residences experienced an extraordinary boom and became one of the clearest indicators of the forces and talents that had been repressed and wasted prior to 1989.*

In order to provide a picture of the extraordinarily dynamic nature of this segment after 1989, we can make use of the general *reflections upon long-term trends in Czech architecture* as expressed by Czech art historian Rostislav Švácha in his theses on the "austerity" of Czech architecture, which we can trace from the late 19th century all the way up to the founder of Czech modern architecture, Jan Kotěra[1].

An assessment of family home construction can be done on a regional basis, where besides Prague we can easily identify other regional centers with a strong tradition of single-family home construction (Liberec, Brno, Olomouc, Zlín, the Ostrava region), as well as projects in spa towns (villas and luxury residences in Karlovy Vary, Mariánské Lázně and similar towns), the Bohemian Forest, Silesia etc., with their much appreciated placement within the natural environment.

No less interesting is an examination of *how some towns came to terms with the rapid political and economic changes and began to build upon their traditions first in the civic realm and subsequently in the construction of quality family homes* (for instance in Litomyšl, where metaphorically speaking "the national revival has not ended" – as expressed in the town's pride and aspirations under the new post-1989 conditions), *in particular by successfully fighting the suburban-style construction of family homes/luxury residences built in the pseudo-style known as the "entrepreneurial baroque."*

At the same time, the family home segment possesses a tangible sense of the tension between culture and technology that has suffused all of architecture in the late modern era, as represented by buildings that deal with environmental issues as radically as possible (traditional and natural materials, local sources, renewability and recycling, minimal impact on nature, etc.) and, on the other extreme, smart houses. Between these two poles, we find a whole range of possibilities and trends. These include low-energy homes, homes that make use of a region's generations of accumulated experience, and modest and seemingly simple structures resulting from a radical approach to the interplay between floor plan, construction, and operations.

No less interesting subjects include the *loosening of the traditional typology of family homes* (which is reflected in the floor plan and interior and exterior), "genre buildings", and the discovery of minimalist residential containers. In terms of technologies, objectives, floor plans, interiors/exteriors, and respect for the natural or urban context, the range of innovative approaches is seemingly endless. In the end effect, however, as it has been for all of history the final result is the work of the architect. Do we in the Czech Republic have architects and projects that can hold their own when compared to the international scene?

In the past two decades, architects and urbanists in the Czech Republic have continued to keep on top of international trends. Compared to the past, in today's "very late modern" era the situation is far more complicated and confusing[/2]. The great thoughts and ideas of modernism – of which one important and highly visible product was Czech functionalism – have been fully realized, exhausted, trivialized or desecrated (cf. pre-fabricated panel housing estates), and emptied of meaning.

Today an enormous amount of information is just a mouse click away, but we lack a useful key for its understanding. At the same time, designs require ever more graphs, visualizations, experience… The architect's work must increasingly and often surprisingly respond to "officialdom", to the characteristics of new materials and the possibilities contained in "parametric design".

In the restless and "agitated culture" at the turn of the millennium, the importance of both individual housing and public space is on the rise. Following the rehabilitation of family luxury homes after 1989, there came the time to rehabilitate public space. The home, house, landscape, and region have become a place for renewal, regeneration, liberation, and becoming aware of fundamental principles.

As a communicative space par excellence, "public space" becomes a place for the shaping of informal, natural contacts and relationships. Individual housing formas a meaningful and necessary counterpoint to this "public space". This is perhaps the best way to understand the *meaning of individual housing – not in the sense of outdoing oneself through ever more demanding architectural and material solutions, but in the sense of being rooted in and working with tradition, with the relationship to place, landscape, region, country.*

This publication consciously presents remarkable and innovative projects that represent a small minority within a flood of banal production. The family homes, villas, and luxury residences captured in the book's photographs and written descriptions do not represent the mainstream, but their significance is uncontested.

They represent projects where the architect's presence is clearly felt – he or she met the client's wishes, fulfilled all the requirements a building should meet (function, economy of operation, ease of repairs, etc.), and respected the local context. The result is a quality building that has become architecture.

The 33 presented projects can be seen as classics – these family homes represent an architecture of enduring value. *We have asked the question: Do we in Czech Republic have architects and projects that can hold their own when compared to the international scene? Does the production of family homes, villas, and luxury residences in the Czech Republic possess qualities and features that can captivate foreign observers and that offer, from their point of view, clearly visible quality? The book's carefully selected representative sample of buildings and its rich photographic documentation invite readers to answer these questions themselves, to actively contribute to the architectural discourse, and perhaps even to share their views with the book's author.*

Adolf Loos, Villa Müller in Prague — Photo: Fotes

Ludwig Mies van der Rohe, Villa Tugendhat in Brno — Photo: David Židlický

1/ Švácha, R.: Czech Architecture and Its Austerity. Fifty Buildings 1989–2004, Prague: Prostor, 2004.

2/ Beneš, O. – Ševčík, O. J.: Architektura: Devadesátá léta a první desítiletí 21. století. Architektura&Urbanizmus, 2011, vol. 45, no. 3-4, pp. 104-135, 30 img., ISSN 0044 8680.

Mladá Boleslav Michalovice / SEA

Author: Petr Suske / www.ateliersea.com /
Design and construction process: 1995 – 2002 | Plot size: 2,566 m² | Building footprint: 123 m²
Photos: Ester Havlová

Few things are more natural than a strawstack in a rural landscape. But what about a strawstack with an umbrella? Why not? After all, we live in the 21st century. The building consists of an outer timber frame with a masonry core. The wooden frame is covered by a 150 mm wall of unfired clay bricks that accumulate heat and have a positive impact on the interior's microclimate. Insulation is via fire-rated straw blocks, separated by a vapor-control layer from the unfired clay bricks. The translucent membrane "umbrella" over the ceiling structure is supported by the chimney at the building's center. The open-plan living space is organized around a central heat-retaining core consisting of the bathrooms, heat source, and chimney. As per the client's request, the bedroom and guest room are separate.

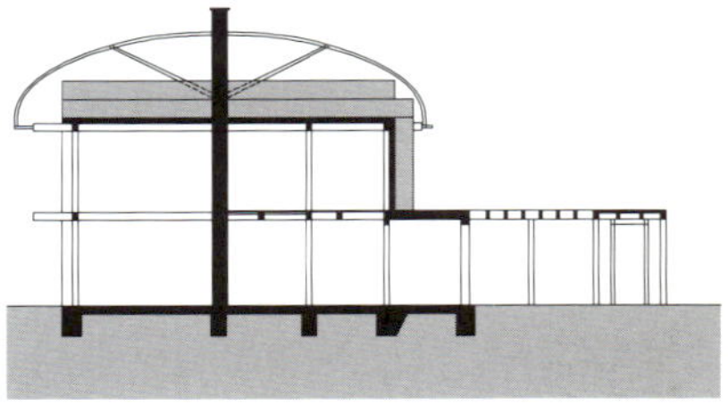

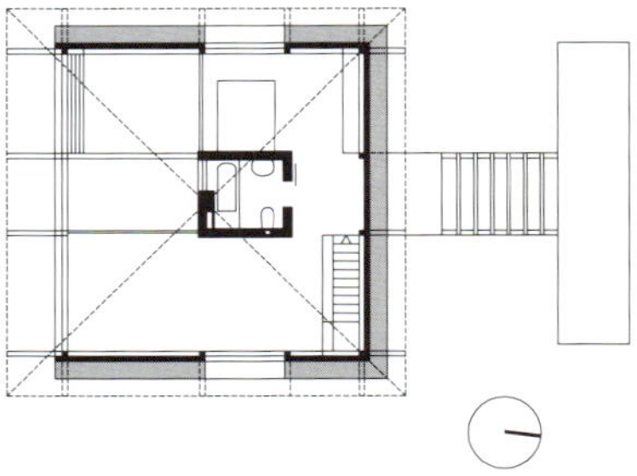

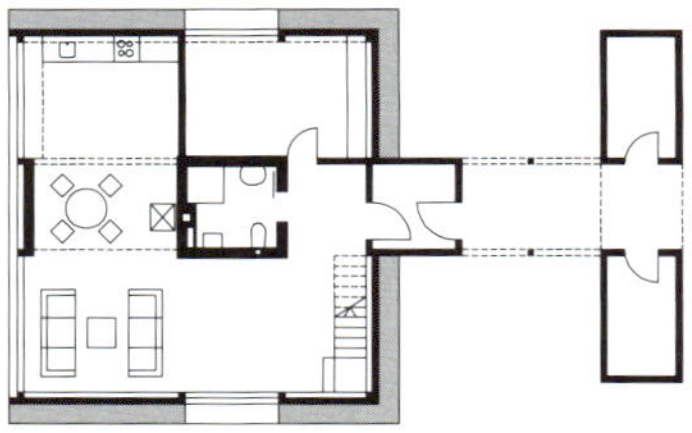

Hráň u Slavonic / Martin Rajniš

Authors: Martin Rajniš, Václav Horecký / www.hutarchitektury.cz /
Design and construction process: 1995 – 2005 | Plot size: 2 566 m² | Built up area: 164 m²
Photos: Andrea Thiel Lhotáková, Radka Cíglerová

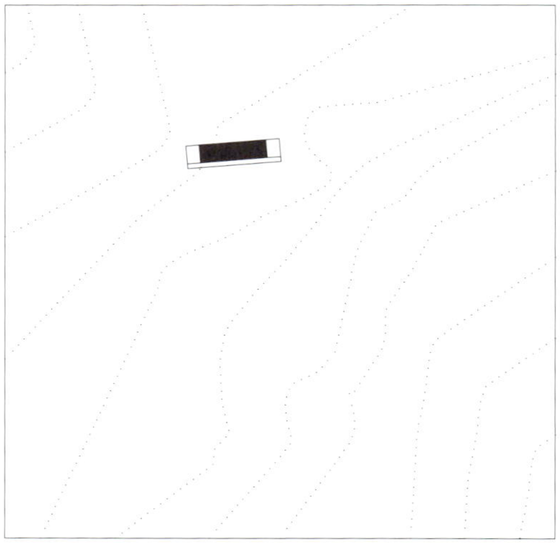

The client purchased land in a protected nature reserve known as "Czech Canada", where he planned to build a cabin among the area's broad meadows and pine-studded rock outcroppings. What emerged is a house consisting of seven 3.60m modules, with the two modules on the edges left open as terraces. The entire northern side is insulated and forms, as in Japan, a long cabinet with sliding doors. The windows on the southern, eastern and western sides of the house are fitted from the inside. The sliding dilation joint allows the fixed swinging double-glazed frames to be fitted into the lumber stack structure, which changes dimensions depending on the wood's dampness or its gradual drying. By experimenting with the use of a hollow lumber stack, the architects have created a fully inhabitable house in which the tectonics of the stack provide pleasant, solid, external shading that prevents the emergence of a greenhouse effect inside the building.

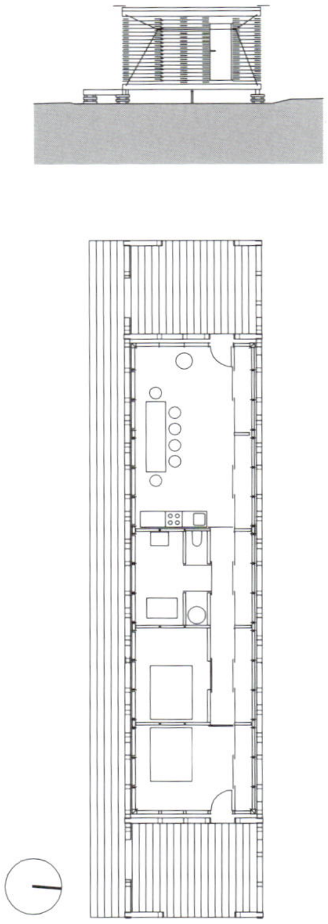

Brno / Zdeněk Fránek

Author: Zdeněk Fránek / www.franekarchitects.cz /
Design and construction process: 1995 – 2005 | Plot size: 3,500 m² | Building footprint: 191 m²
Photos: Filip Šlapal, Ester Havlová

The building's disadvantageous orientation on a steep north-facing slope resulted in a design that allowed a narrow strip of light to pass through the house. The surrounding greenery filters and refines the light entering the house. This precise dosing of light offers a new benefit: the intense experience of having a view of the dense vegetation on Červený kopec hill and a panoramic view of the city. The house is built using a combination of masonry and poured concrete. The conical section above the garage forms the main living spaces on a level directly accessible from both sides, thus seamlessly connecting the interior and exterior. One highlight of the house is its garden with an apricot orchard, a terrace, two concrete caves and an acacia jungle on the upper part of the property.

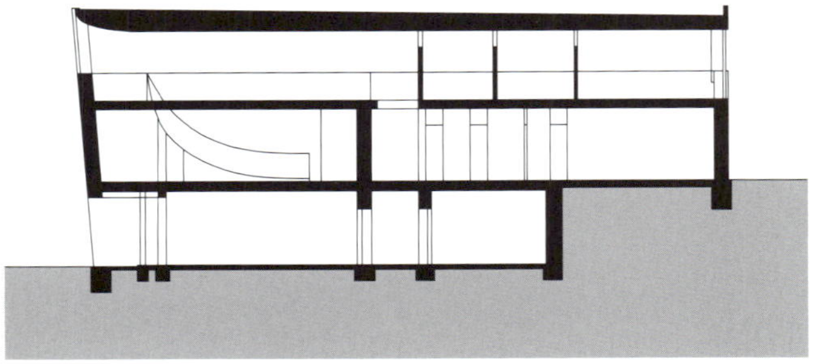

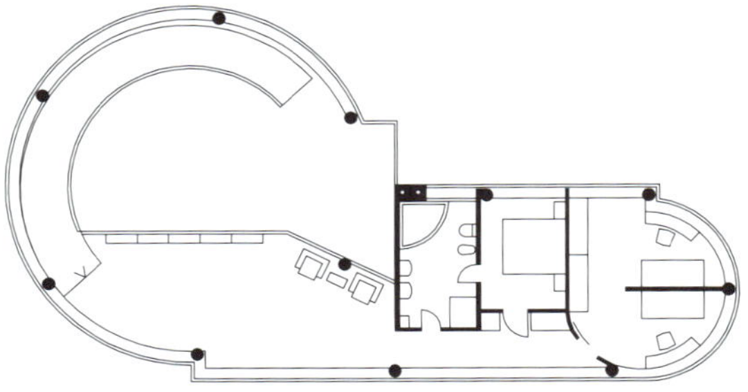

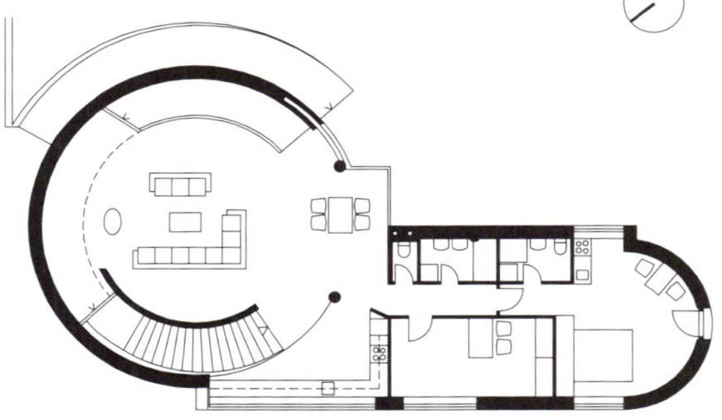
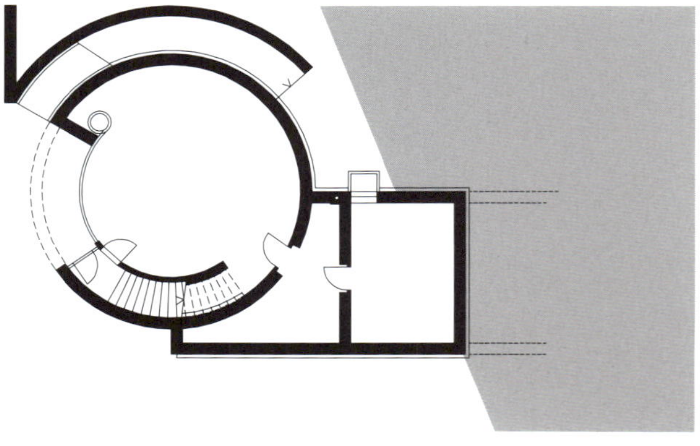

Brno / Petr Pelčák

Author: Petr Pelčák / www.pelcak.cz /
Design and construction process: 1999 – 2003 | Plot size: 1,594 m^2 | Building footprint: 135 m^2
Photos: Filip Šlapal

The ultimate goal was to create a modestly sized family house that would nevertheless be generous in terms of living spaces. This goal was achieved through simplicity and proportions, by linking the building with the terrain, and by making use of the site's panoramic views. The outer dimensions of the building, which is located on a steep south-facing slope, are 7×11 meters. From the outside, the main residential part of the building is covered in plaster; the rear part set into the rocky slope and housing the utilities rooms is clad in local stone. The plot is located in the warmest part of the city of Brno, which partially inspired the building's architecture with the use of vertical as well as horizontal ceramic structures.

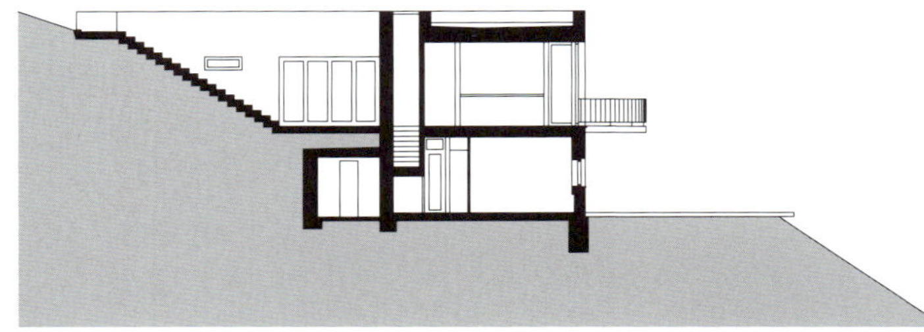

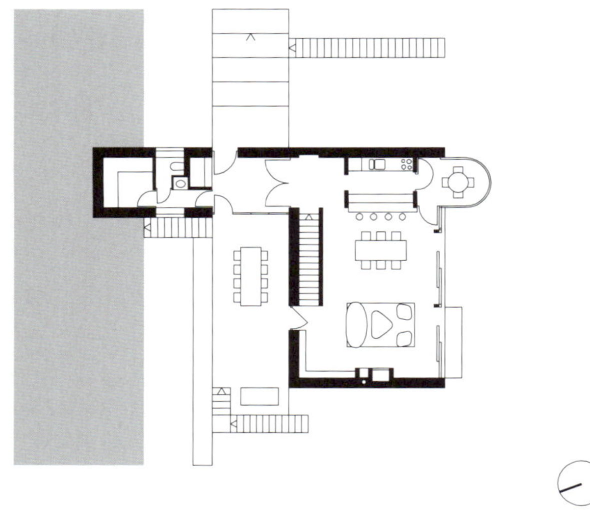

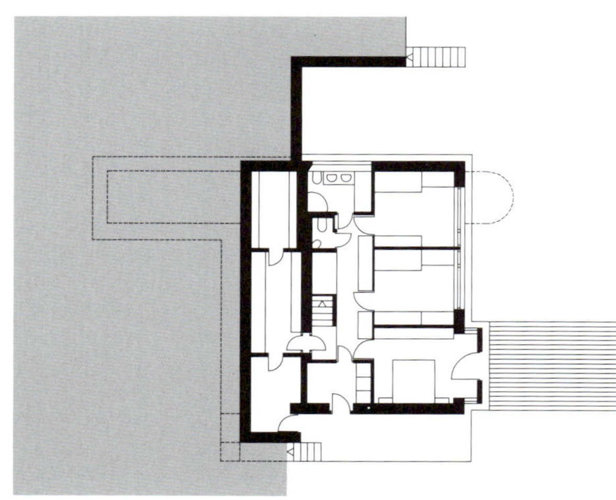

Beroun / HŠH architekti

Authors: Petr Hájek, Tomáš Hradečný, Jan Šépka / www.hsharchitekti.cz /
Design and construction process: 2001 – 2004 | Plot size: 1751 m² | Building footprint: 108 m²
Photos : Pavel Pszczolka

In 2001, the architect and client engaged in abstract discussions on space that eventually gave rise to something like a Spatial Frame or Spatial Grid. The building is like a fragment of a spatial macrostructure – a network of 6×2×2 modules or cubes (24 in total), an abstract frame into which the home's various functions are organized. Each cube represents an independent volume unit with a particular function attached. The building consists of an assembled steel skeleton with a concrete-and-glass facade. It is essentially a building kit with a load-bearing modular cube measuring 3m on each side. There is no main facade; there is no hierarchy. All the parts are connected using the same system. There are no indoor hallways. The rooms are connected in various ways, thus adding to the building's rich variety. This approach also allows for truly flexible use of the building.

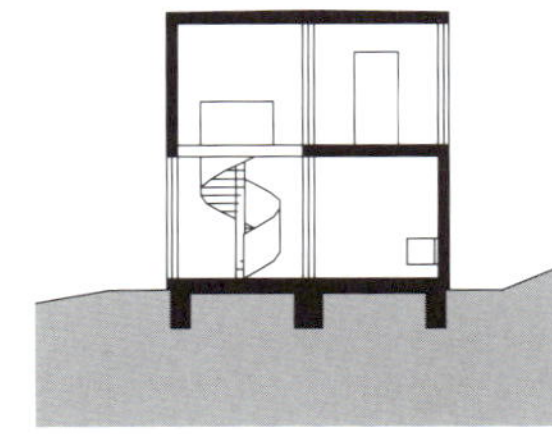

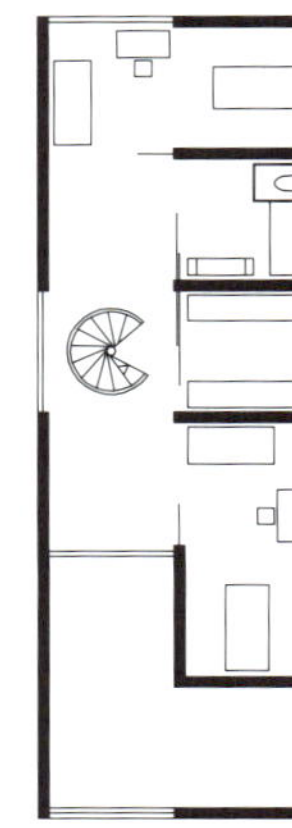

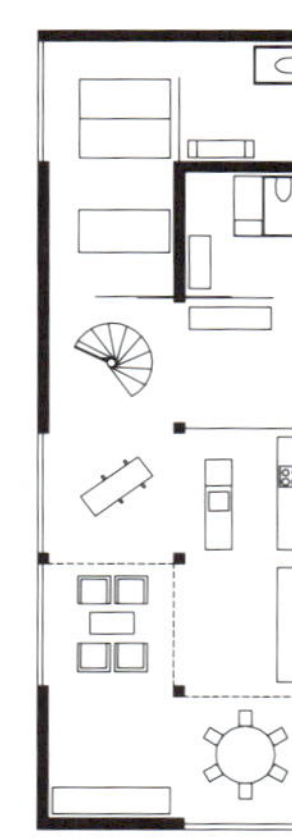

Semilsko / Rak, Raková, Rydlo, Skalický

Authors: Milan Rak, Iveta Raková, Libor Rydlo, Alexandr Skalický / www.archteam.cz / www.a-skalicky.cz /
Design and construction process: 2001 – 2006 | Plot size: 18,630 m^2 | Building footprint: 108 m^2
Photos: Ester Havlová

Located in an area close to the mountains, the building's scale and character reflect the dispersed rural nature of the local housing. The interior spaces communicate with the landscape via large windowpanes. One distinctive feature of the house is its covered veranda with a view of the mountains. The interior – an open space defined only by the outer walls – consists of a live-in studio with a gallery in the attic. All utility and technical rooms are arranged within a closed block at the far end of the house. The wooden shed running along the building's entire length provides covered parking and acts as a terrace. The house is an easily assembled timber frame building with a facade consisting of insulating aluminum panels. The use of timber framing prevails in the interior as well, with the final surface inside and outside covered in aluminum cladding.

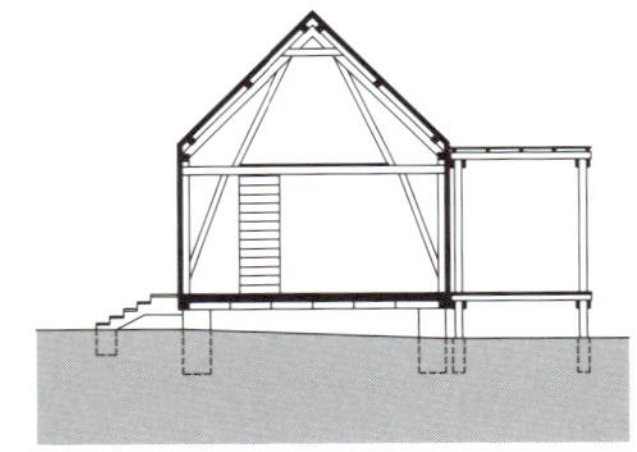
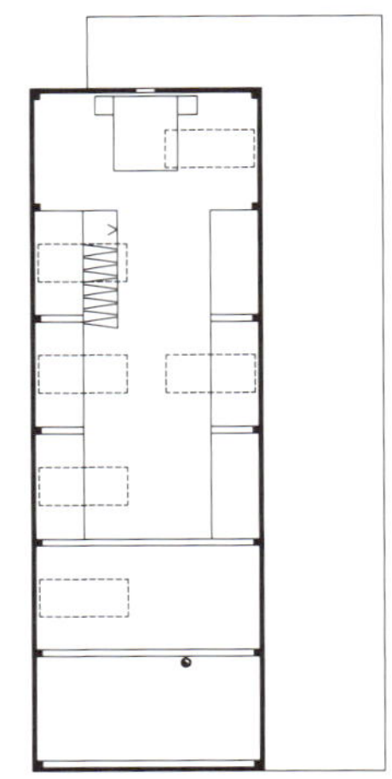
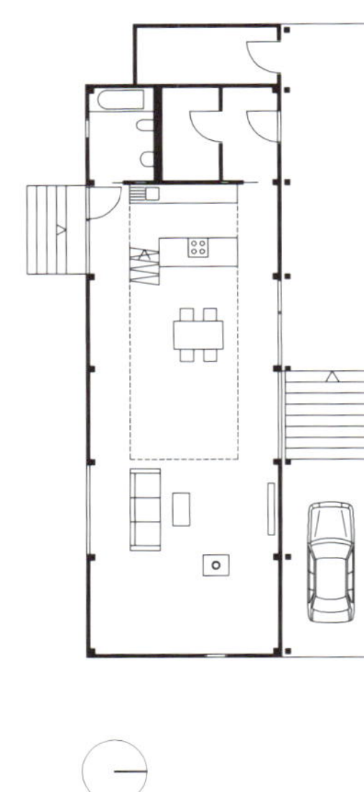

Praha-Liboc / L&P Architektonický ateliér

Author: Jan Línek / www.arch.cz/linek /

Design and construction process: 2002 – 2006 | Plot size: 1,497 m^2 | Building footprint: 242 m^2

Photos: Filip Šlapal

Located close to the former Hvězda royal game reserve, the building's site posed a great challenge. The site and the clients' openness to the architect's experimentation resulted in a building that fits well into the existing urban fabric of the Liboc district. The building appears austere from the northern, street-facing side, but opens up towards the garden on the opposite side. Its two sections are joined by a narrow glass-covered strip. The larger section with the main living area is on the same level as the garden. A painting studio below the roof is connected to the garden via a bridge. The house is divided into a man's area with main living room and kitchen, private rooms, a steam room, whirlpool, bathroom, bedroom, and office; and a section for the woman of the house with a studio, bedroom, and bathroom. The two areas are connected via a glass bridge across the narrow strip between the two sections. Sliding colored panels on the south facade create a variety of lighting spectrums while changing the interior mood.

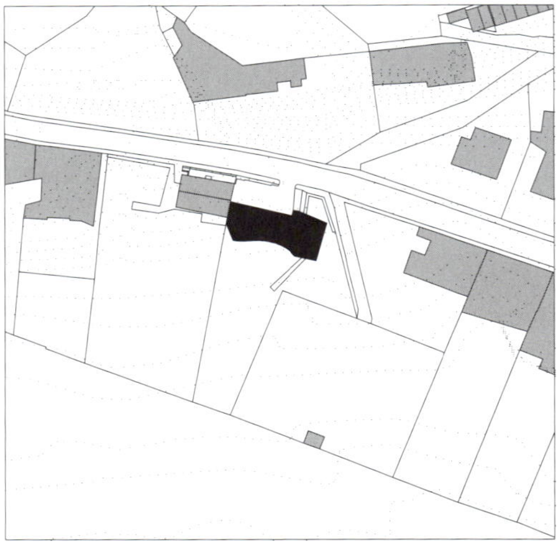

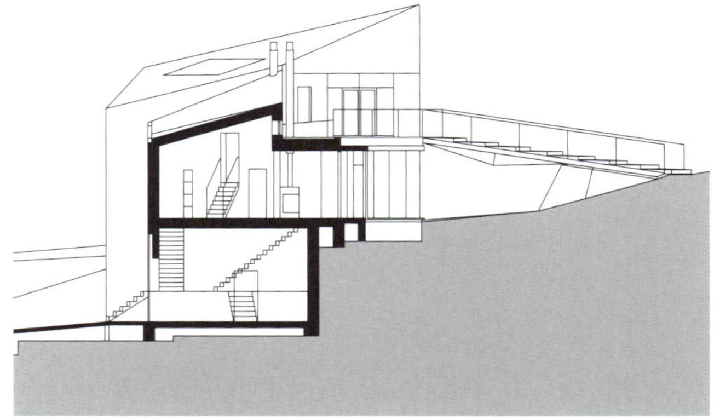

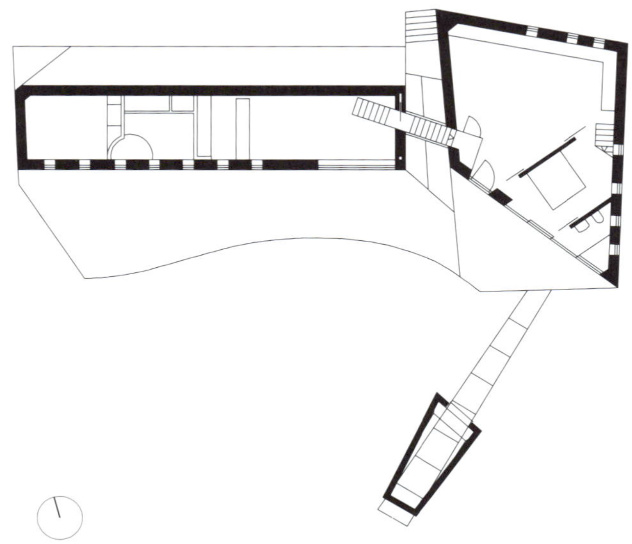

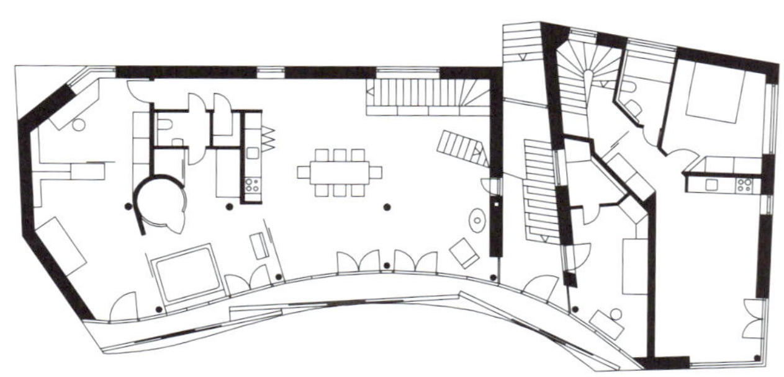

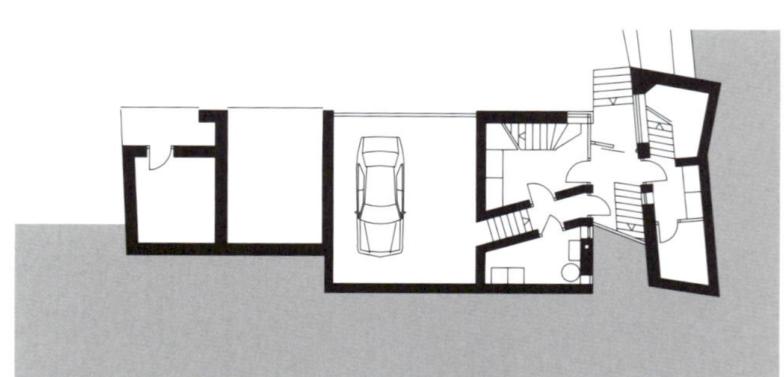

Nespeky / Ladislav Lábus AA

Authors: Ladislav Lábus, Marek Nábělek / www.archiweb.cz /
Design and construction process: 2002 – 2008 | Plot size: 3,163 m^2 | Building footprint: 205 m^2
Photos: Tomáš Balej

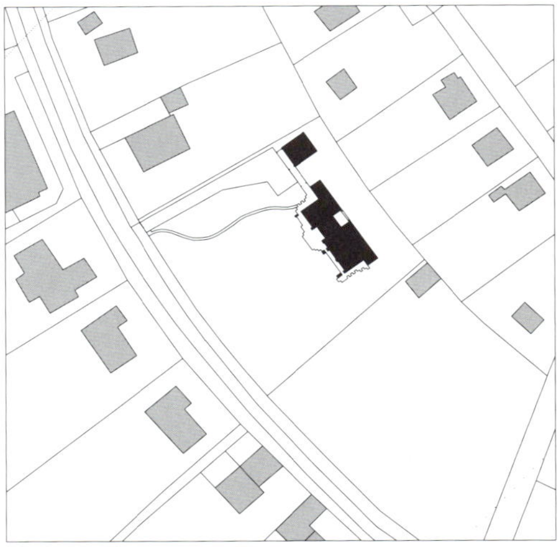

The client requested a single-story building of relatively small dimensions. The house was designed with a view towards the optimal usage of the plot and existing greenery. The architect situated the house towards the rear of the plot, with a view of the garden and the hills rising over the river. The objective of connecting the interior and exterior while extending the house into the garden has been taken to the extreme: the villa is more garden house than residential building. The boundaries between interior and exterior have been suppressed in the floors, load-bearing walls, window design and ceilings, and in the building's entire approach to space and volume. The various elements' simple design further adds to this feeling, as do the surface finish and choice of natural materials.

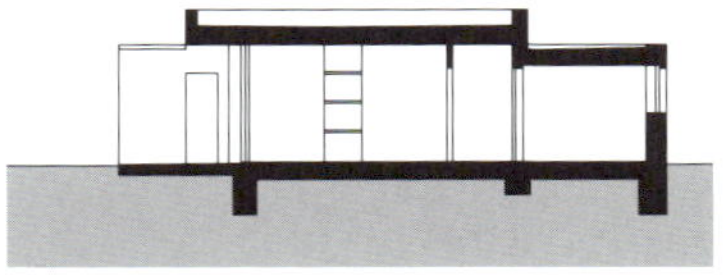

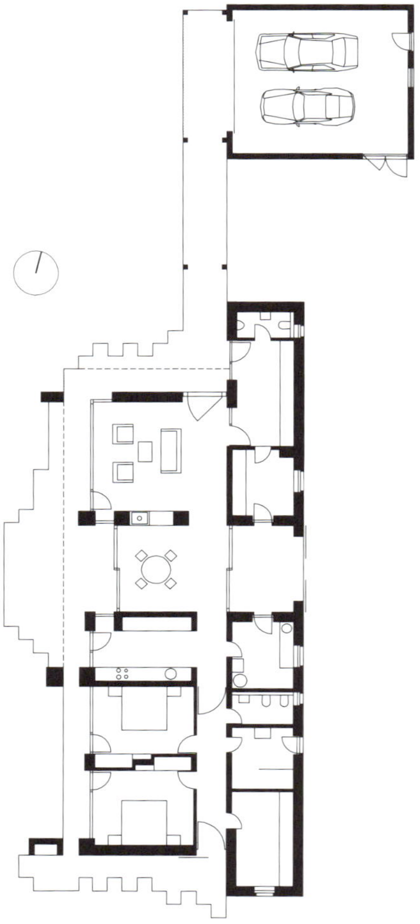

Zdiměřice / FIALA+NEMEC s.r.o.

Author: Stanislav Fiala with Milan Bulva, Daniela Polubědovová, Jiří Václavů / www.fialanemec.com / Design and construction process: 2003 – 2007 | Plot size: 931 m² | Building footprint: 333 m²
Photos: Filip Šlapal

A house as a memory from visiting the Saharan Berbers. The nearly square floor plan possesses an organically shaped inner bay that brings the garden into the interior. Colorful blossoming greenery turns the entire site into one clearly organized system. Wild trees are kept behind a fence and illuminated by reflectors to create a calming scene. The bay can be fully enclosed using moving panels made of woven-willow trellises. The flexible material and color design respond to the client's needs. The home's true showpiece, however, is its technical equipment. The heating and cooling systems are based on a combination of heat pump and solar collectors and use wall and ceiling heating to cool the building in summer, thus allowing it to breathe.

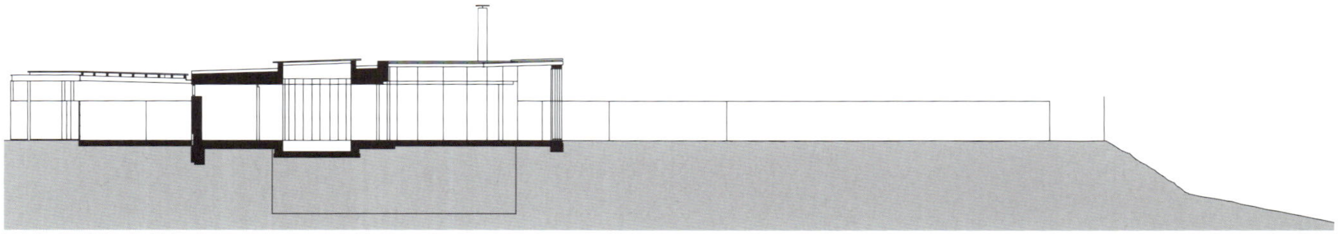

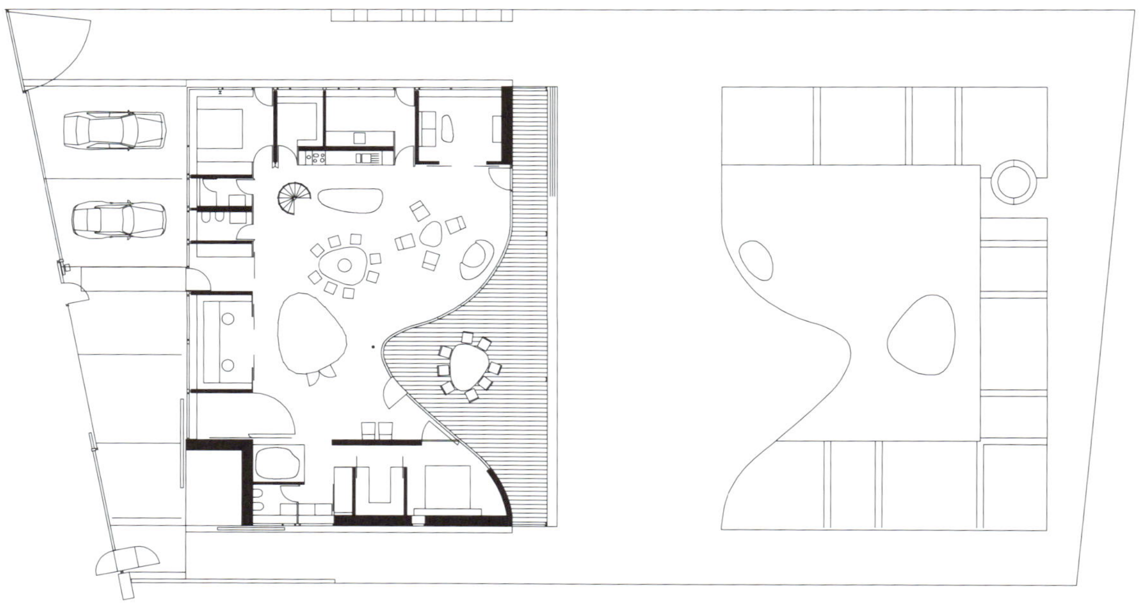

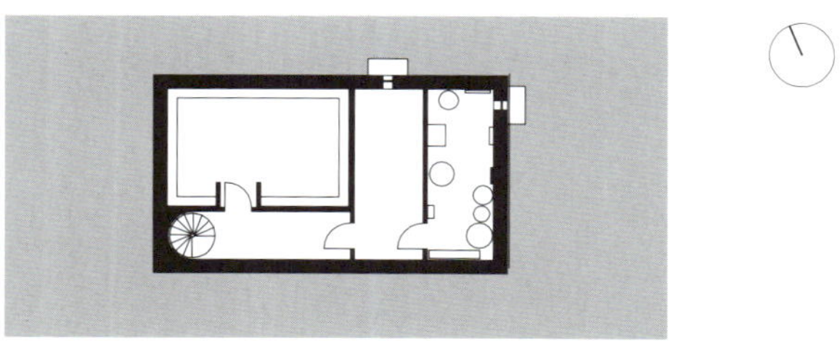

Jičín / Roman Koucký architektonická kancelář s.r.o.

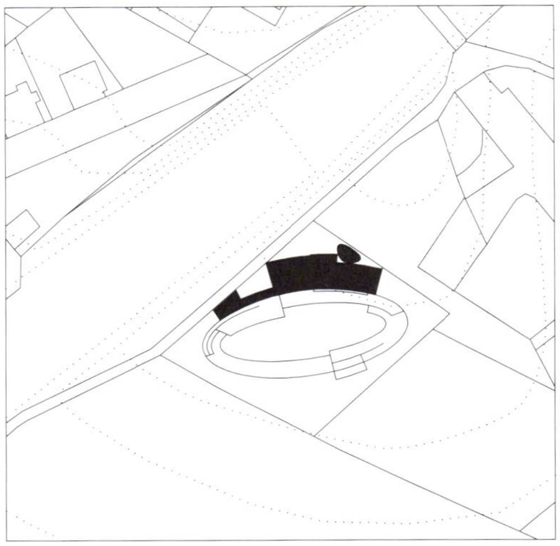

Authors: Roman Koucký, Šárka Malá, Libor Kábrt / www.koucky-arch.cz /
Design and construction process: 2003 – 2011 | Plot size: 2,400 m^2 | Building footprint: 278 m^2
Photos : Ester Havlová

Working with a slightly rhomboid-shaped site, the architects created an elliptical inner garden that defines the project's other elements. The house forms one side of the garden perimeter, with its outer facade – a concrete flower-covered retaining wall – also defining the property's northern and western boundary. The plot's remaining edges are shielded by a wall of trees, with the house wrapping itself around the green elliptical space. The building's interior spaces rise slowly in height as we move away from the entrance. Along the rounded facade, all the spaces are connected by a band of glass walls to create a sense of connection and belonging. Hidden in the ground between the house and the retaining wall is a swimming pool with small sparkling roof lights. A small light shaft carved into the embankment behind the kitchen provides the main living area with additional light, air, and space.

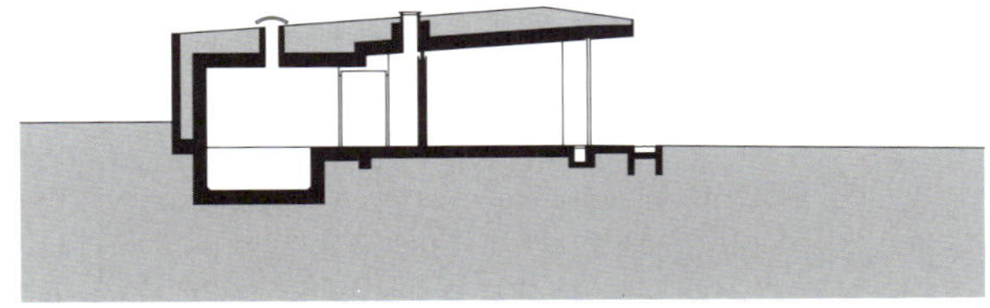

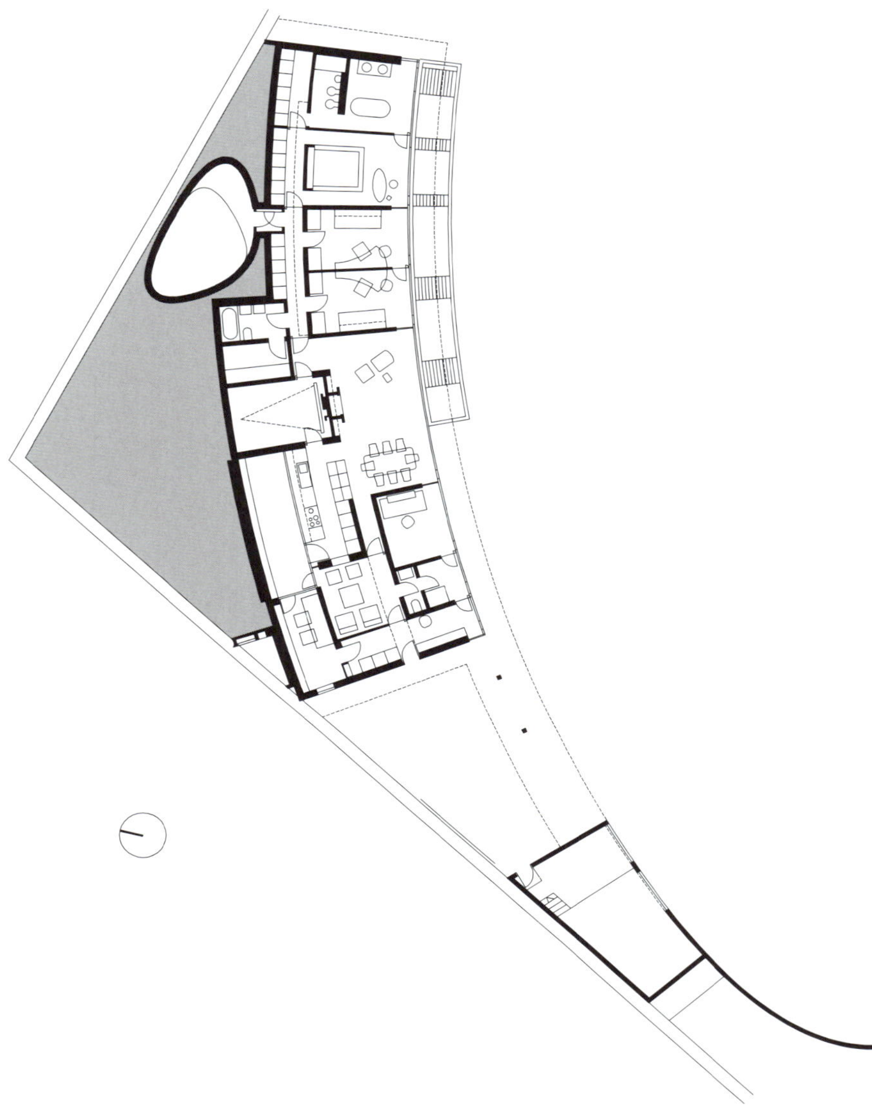

Humpolec / OK PLAN ARCHITECTS

Authors: Luděk Rýzner, Marcela Kostková / www.okplan.cz /
Design and construction process: 2004 – 2005 | Plot size: 430 m^2 | Building footprint: 72 m^2
Photos: Jan Malý

The building was completed on a site close to the center of the town of Humpolec on a long, narrow, and mildly sloping plot of 430 m2 (including the building footprint). The site was sold to the client as one that would be difficult to build on. The building design respects the existing street frontage and responds to the existing heights of the nearby buildings. The structural skeleton is made of a galvanized steel frame in a 6×6×3m grid, with all structural elements exposed in the interior: steel beams, trapezoidal profiles, concrete blocks, concrete floors. The building is clad in 4mm-thick Corten sheets, with Profilit glass panels on the first floor. The building's facade even gave it its local nickname, "Tin Can". The interior is furnished with unconventional particle board furniture painted in a white semi-gloss finish.

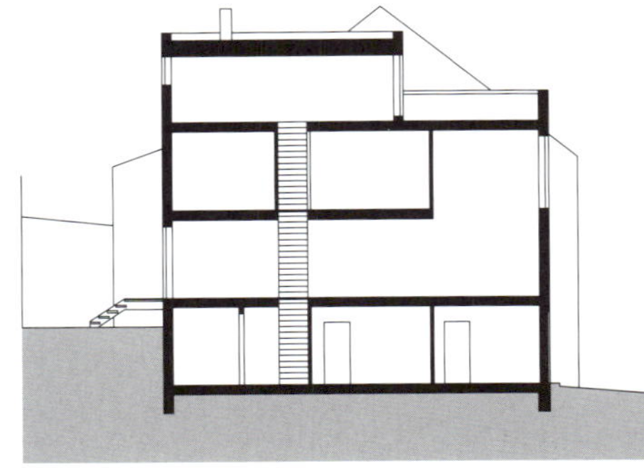

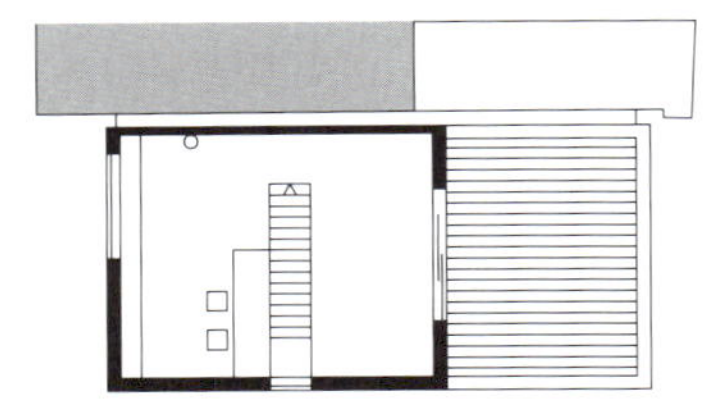

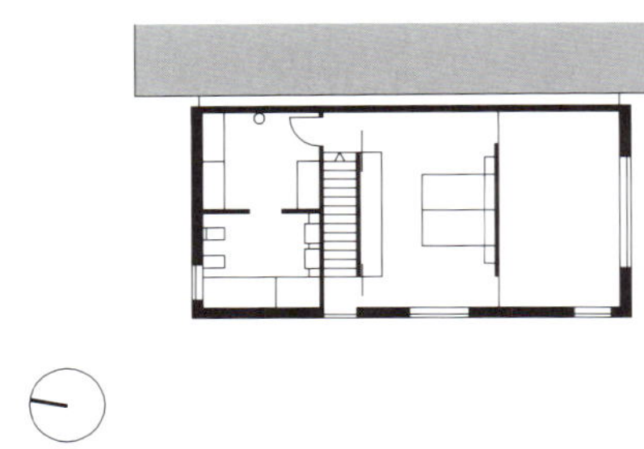

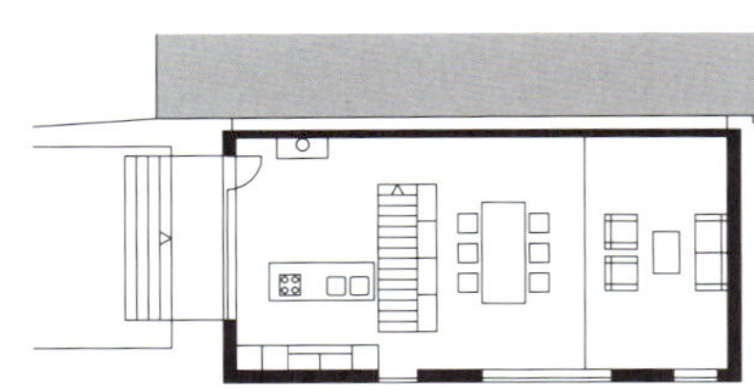

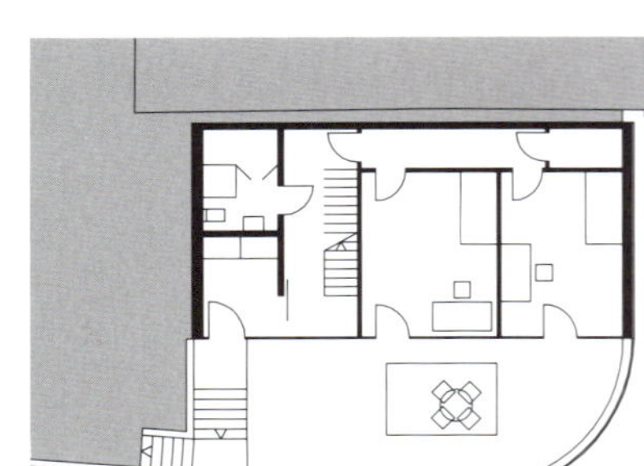

Květnice / KA architects

Author: Kamila Amblerová / www.ka-architekti.cz /
Design and construction process: 2004 – 2006 | Plot size: 860 m² | Building footprint: 133 m²
Photos : Andrea Thiel Lhotáková

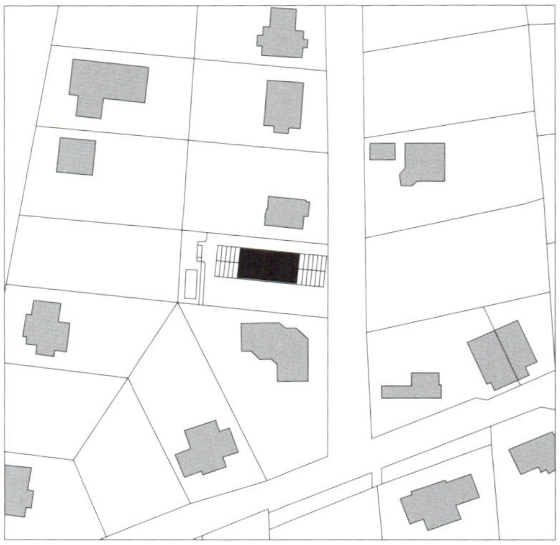

The house was built on a site that, as a result of the construction of many houses around it, suddenly suffered from a lack of greenery. The building's main architectural feature is the wooden frame passing fluidly from the interior to the exterior to form a primary outer structure for climbing plants. On the roof level, this frame extends over the glass facades and the seating below the pergola in order to visually connect the interior and exterior spaces. The outer structures form an intermediate space. The building's first floor is built of brickwork with the bare masonry exposed in the main interior living space. The brickwork is topped by a visible reinforced-concrete ring-beam. The rest of the building is wooden, with the frame structure exposed. The gables and southern facades are glazed, and the facade is ventilated and clad in mountain larch.

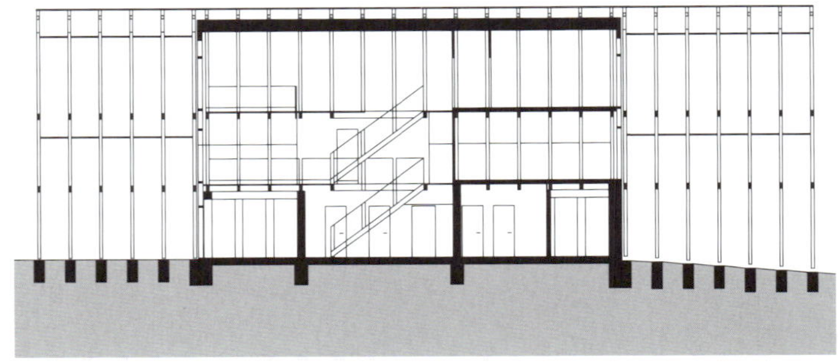

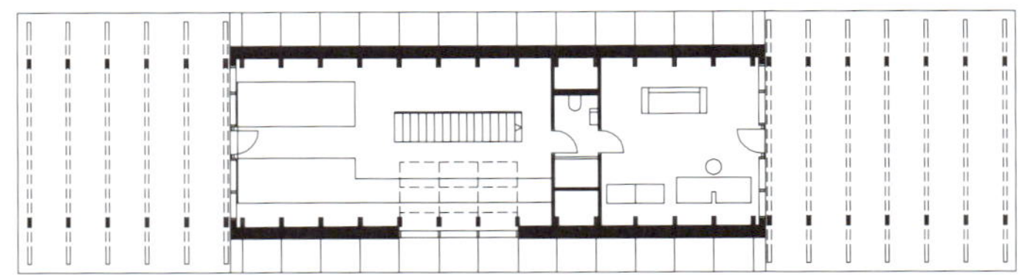

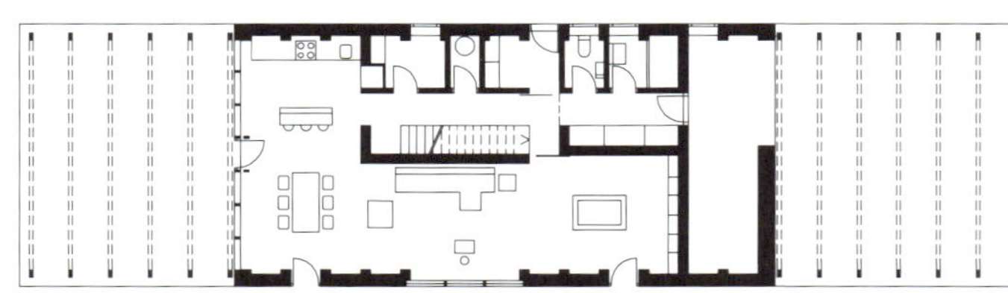

Posázaví / sporadical architektonická kancelář

Authors: Aleš Kubalík, Josef Kocián, Jakub Našinec, Veronika Sávová / www.sporadical.cz /
Design and construction process: 2004 – 2007 | Plot size: 15,700 m² | Building footprint: 74 m²
Photos: Ester Havlová, Jan Kuděj

The house is situated at the top of a north-facing slope in a former 1.57-hectare tree park. The ground floor was designed as one single room with a central core containing a kitchen, utility rooms, storage areas, a staircase and a fireplace. Sliding walls enable the kitchen to be separated from the southern hallway, which can be used as a winter garden. The use of a central core makes it possible to open up the surrounding spaces in order to offer panoramic views of the surrounding landscape. The upper floor is a self-contained quiet area. The bedrooms have narrow windows with distinct views onto the garden. A large window above the bath frames a view onto the crowns of the trees. A "secret" staircase leads along the facade from one bedroom onto a roof terrace for leisure and relaxation. Natural shading from a large oak tree, combined with a parapet running along the circumference of the roof, creates a hidden intimate place under the open sky.

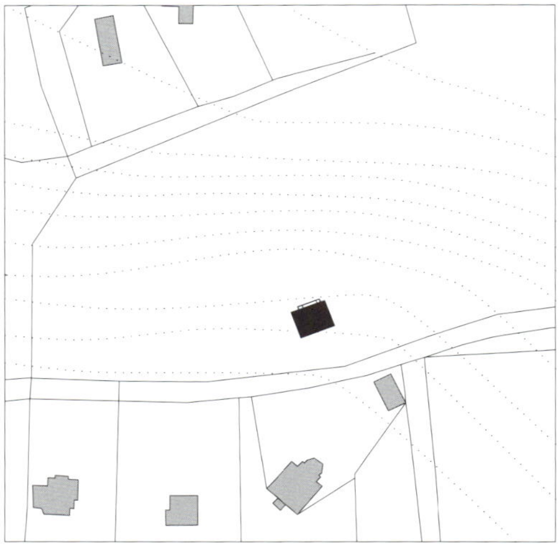

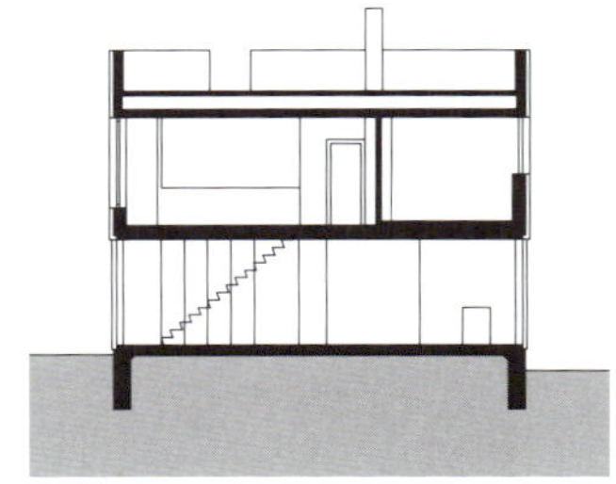

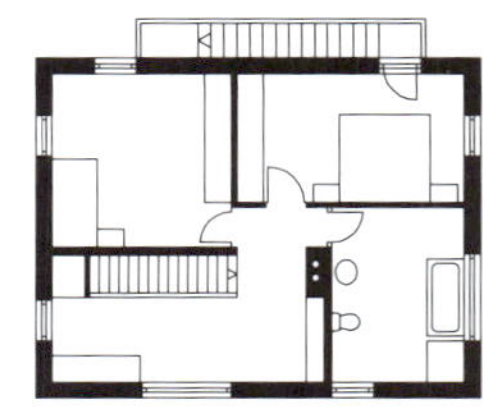

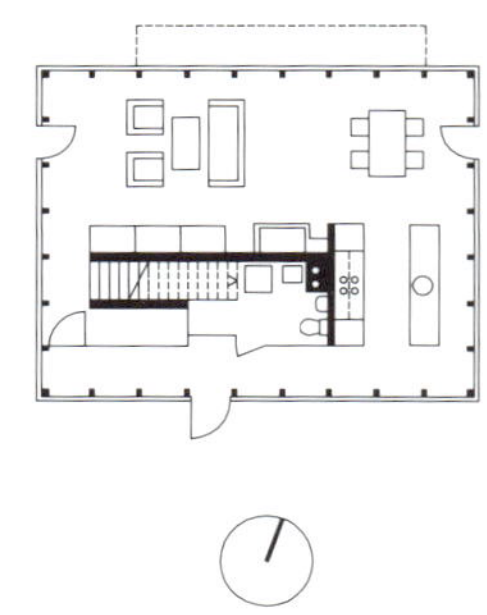

Zadní Třebaň / Sodomková Sodomka Architekti

Authors: Šárka Sodomková, Marek Sodomka / www.sodomka-architekti.cz /
Design and construction process: 2004 – 2007 | Plot size (two times): 650 m² | Building footprint: 103 m²
Photos: Ester Havlová

The two buildings' unconventional vertical stratification resulted from the site's characteristics: narrow, located on a sloping wooded terrain overlooking the romantic Berounka River valley, and with little sunlight. The kitchens and outdoor terraces are situated on the upper level at the site's best location. Additional south-facing windows over the northern part of the living spaces bring the sun's rays inside even in December and January, when the sun is usually hidden behind the hillside horizon. The bedrooms on the lowest level remain cool even on the hottest summer days. Since the site could not be reached by heavy machinery, the houses are supported on micropiles built using a portable kit that can be carried by a single person. The steel stilts support the building's timber frame, which is exposed in the interior, where it serves as shelves. The fir floors, spruce walls and larch facade give off a pleasant fragrance. The large frameless windows accentuate the beauty of the river-valley view.

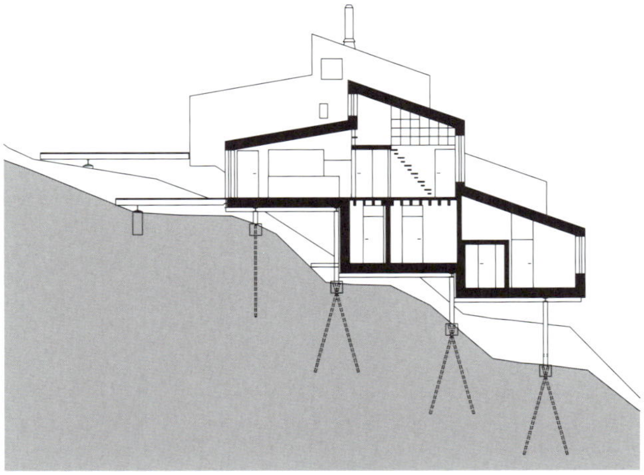

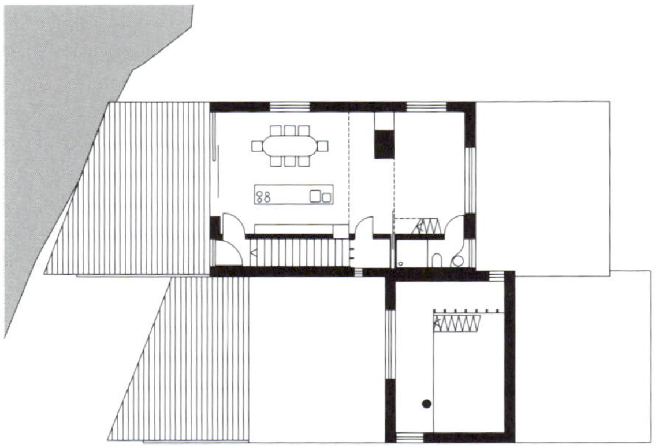

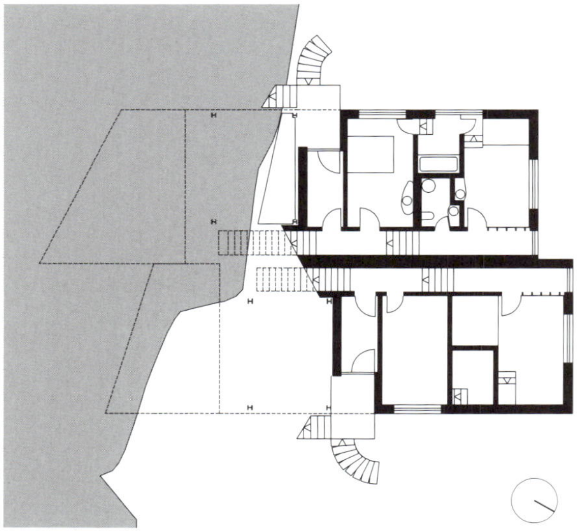

Brno-Žebětín / Makovsky & partners

Authors: Zdeněk Makovský, Daniel Makovský / www.makovsky.eu /
Design and construction process: 2006 – 2008 | Plot size (2x): 429 m^2 | Building footprint: 195 m^2
Photos: Manfred Seidel, Adam Sirotek

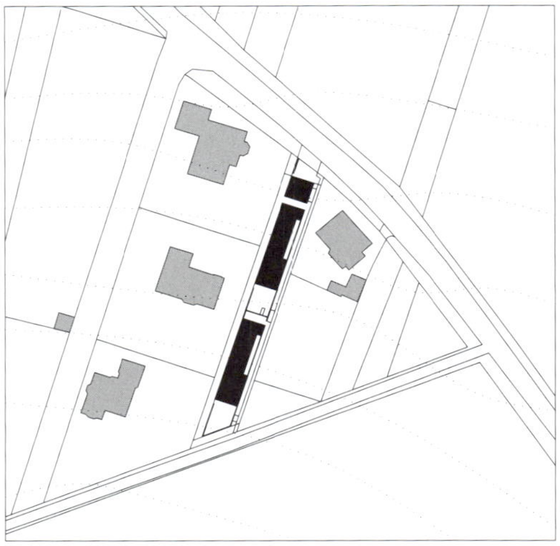

The two houses, built on a slightly sloping plot near the local cemetery, are partially recessed into the hillside. Their layout responds to the plot's unfavorable dimensions and orientation. Because regulations require the buildings to be a particular distance from the neighboring plots, both single-floor houses' outer walls are without windows. Instead, they receive daylight via enclosed atria. The main entrances are from the northern atria. The quiet zone with bedrooms and bathrooms is accessible from the corridor running along the western wall. The living room with kitchen opens up towards the southern atrium surrounded by concrete walls. The buildings are made of thermal insulating cast-in-situ architectural concrete. The walls and roofs are made of a single layer of the same material, 450 and 650mm. The inner walls and atrium walls are made of regular architectural concrete, as are the floors and other interior and exterior concrete elements.

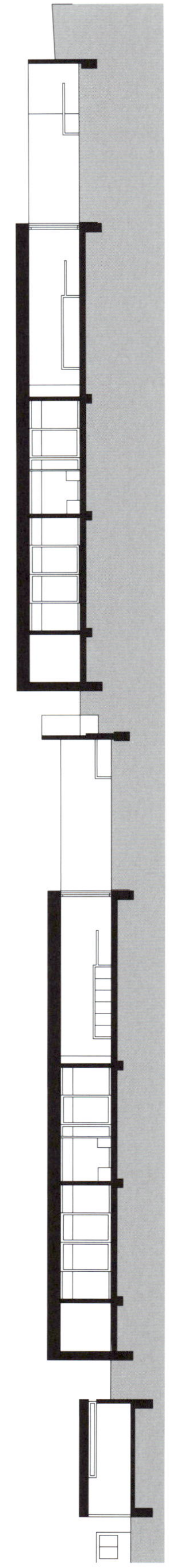

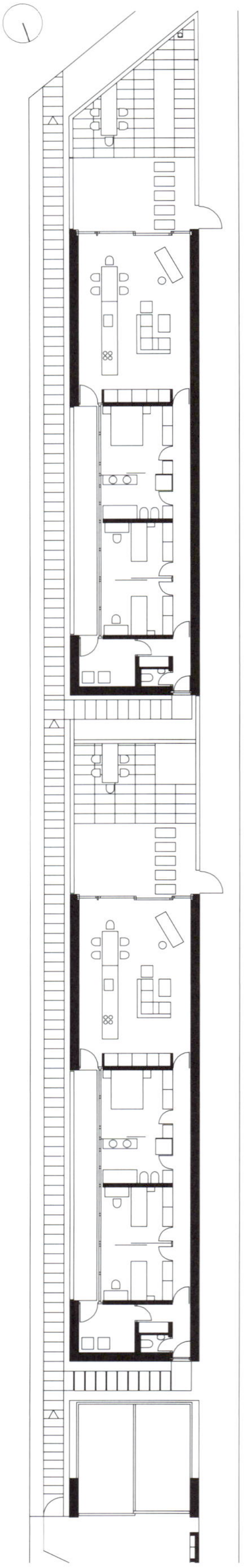

Kojetín / Kamil Mrva Architects

Authors: Kamil Mrva, B. Bebek, J. Holub, J. Pospíšilová, R. Leskovjan / www.mrva.net /
Design and construction process: 2006 – 2009 | Plot size: 3,440 m² | Building footprint: 134 m²
Photos: Studio TOAST

The house stands on a hill with a view in the middle of Kojetín near Nový Jičín. The client's objective was to first convert an old barn into living spaces and to build a house nearby in the future. The newly built studio has been inserted into the original barn, using the existing stone walls and posts from the year 1862. The inner wooden structure opens to the west and south via large glass windows. The idea of building one large space with a kitchen, dining room, seating area and office, bedroom, and bathroom originated from the historical dwelling types found in the region, where all activities happen in one room. The outer terrace consists of a sheltered part for summer relaxation and a summer deck that extends further out. The load-bearing frame and lightweight roof are made of timber, the ventilated facade is made of plywood boards, and the windows are double-glazed with aluminum frames and facade shades.

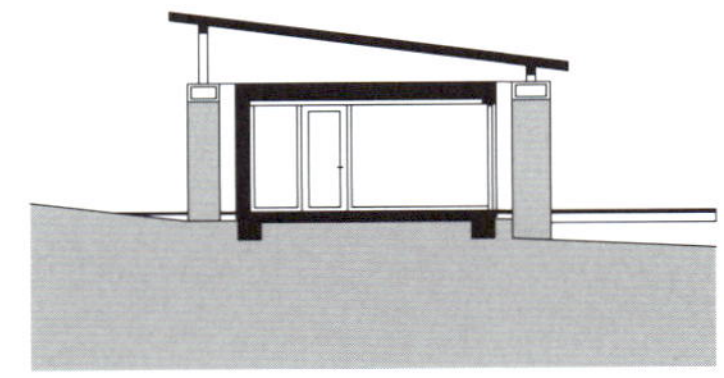

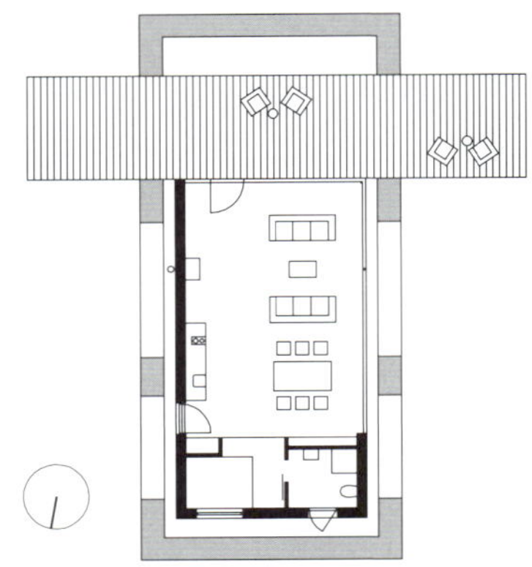

Kuřim / knesl+kynčl architekti

Authors: Jiří Knesl, Jakub Kynčl, Václav Štojdl / www.knesl-kyncl.com /
Design and construction process: 2006 – 2009 | Plot size: 2,055 m² | Building footprint: 125 m²
Photos: Tomáš Rasl

This single-generation home is located at the foot of Horka Hill in the northwestern part of the town of Kuřim. The rectangular three-story building was inserted perpendicular to the steep southeast-oriented slope with a view of town. The interior spaces on each floor have been carved into the building's compact mass in such a way that the final form provides comfortable living conditions in terms of use, lighting and orientation. Each floor is devoted to one specific function: the partly sunken ground floor contains entrance spaces, a garage and utilities rooms; the middle floor houses social spaces; and the private rooms are located on the building's top floor. All living spaces have access to one of the terraces and the garden. The house was designed using masonry walls and reinforced concrete ceilings; the outer walls are sandwich walls with a layer of natural facing bricks.

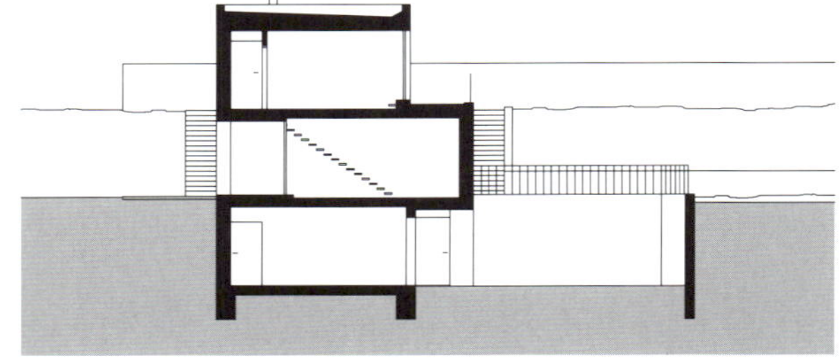

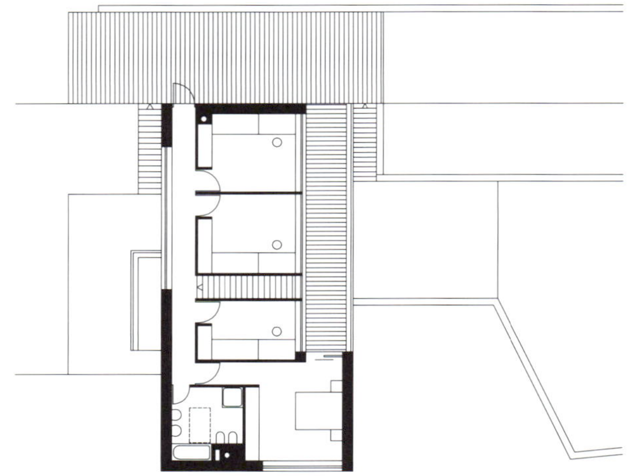

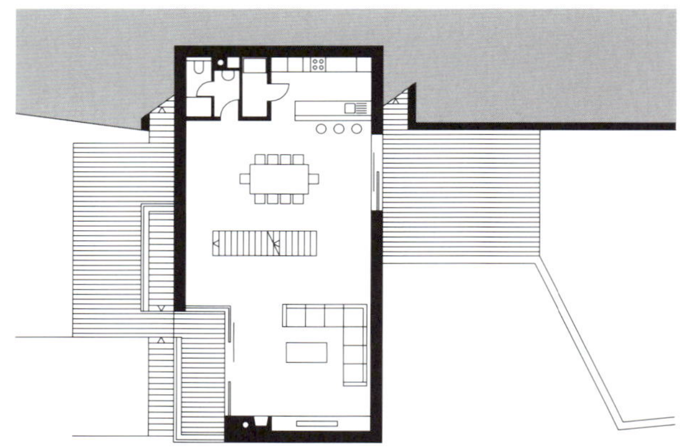

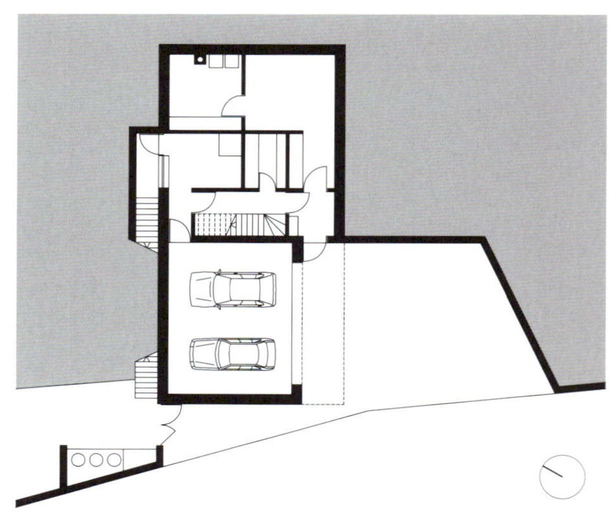

Prague / Šrámková architekti

Authors: Lukáš Ehl, Tomáš Koumar, Alena Šrámková / www.alenasramkova.cz /
Design and construction process: 2006 – 2013 | Plot size: 659 m^2 | Building footprint: 102 m^2
Photos: Rudolf Skopec

This house for a family of four was built on an irregular trapezoidal plot that slopes mildly towards the northeast. The southwestern part of the property is raised 4 – 6m above the remaining site, thus forming a natural interface with the Drahaň nature park. The simple rectangular block is partially sunk into the terrain, with an underground garage attached to the basement from the east, separated by an expansion joint. On the upper floor is an open-plan living area with a kitchen and toilet. On the ground floor are the entrance and three bedrooms with shared bathroom, and the basement is home to a studio apartment (office), utility rooms and a two-car garage. The various floors are reached via a straight stairway along the southeast facade or an elevator in the building's corner. The house is a reinforced concrete structure with an outer layer of natural facing bricks. The retaining walls and garage are made of exposed concrete.

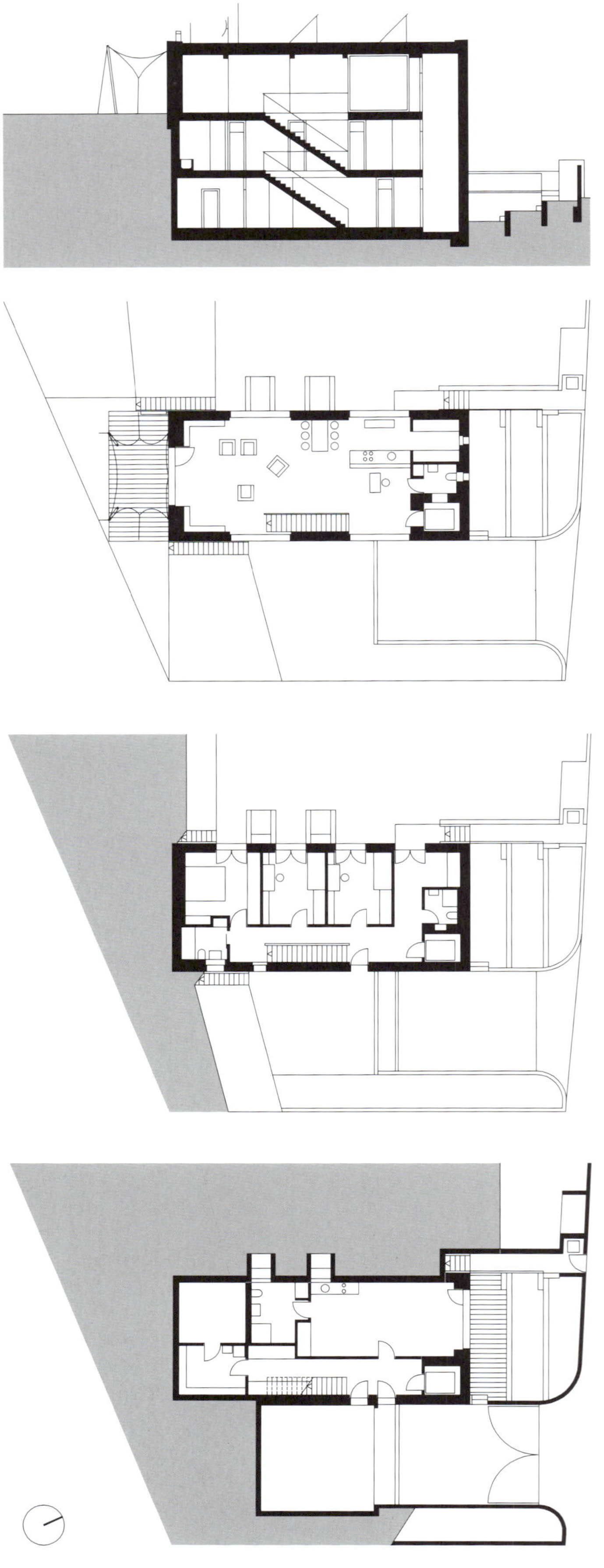

Brno / Kuba & Pilař architekti

Authors: Tomáš Pilař, Vít Košťál, Ladislav Kuba / www.arch.cz/kuba.pilar /
Design and construction process: 2006 – 2013 | Plot size: 360 m² | Building footprint: 110 m²
Photos: David Židlický

Designed on a narrow rectangular footprint, the building's basic shape is a rectangle from which several spaces have been "removed". The biggest such "removed" volume is a vertical atrium that divides the house into two parts. The remaining "removed" spaces consist of covered balconies ("loggias") and terraces. The living areas are oriented towards the west onto a river valley and into the central atrium. The house is enclosed by a frame that provides shade while retaining the building's basic rectangular shape. Openings in the semi-transparent facade reflect the building's interior layout, with the facade material extending over the recessed balconies as railings and defining the rooftop terrace on the third floor. The shade cover is made of a black steel grate, and the outer glass-covered balcony cladding is also black. Most indoor structural elements and materials are white – wall plaster, polyurethane flooring, aluminum windows, and steel staircase.

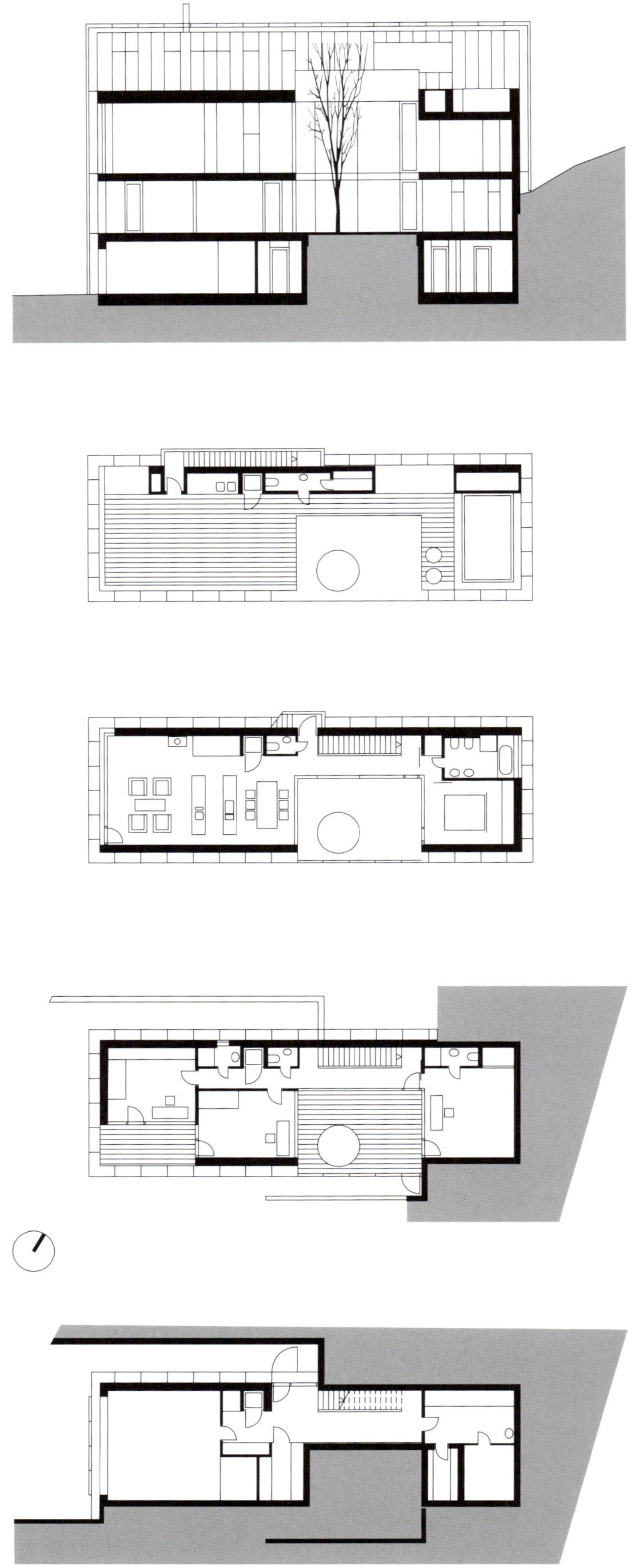

Králův Dvůr / OV-A

Authors: Jiří Opočenský, Štěpán Valouch / www.ov-a.cz / garden Martina Vlnasova / www.a05.cz / Design and construction process: 2007 – 2009 | Plot size: 1,212 m² | Building footprint: 188 m²
Photos: Tomáš Souček, Jakub Vlček

The building is located in a small newly built area at the edge of town. The sloping site, which offers beautiful views, rises towards a long cemetery wall by a church. The new home for a five-member family was built strictly on one level, with everybody given close access to the main living space. Built in the middle of a garden with no fence, the single-story rectangular building resembles a garden pavilion. The three private sections with bedrooms and utilities combine to define the building's "public space", which transitions smoothly via covered terraces to the exterior. Instead of a fence along the property's edge, privacy is provided by translucent larch window shutters that wrap all the way around the building's facade. When the shutters are closed, the terraces become extra rooms that expand the building's interior. The foundation slab supports a frame of wooden beams with mineral-wool infill. The glass walls are constructed using an aluminum facade system.

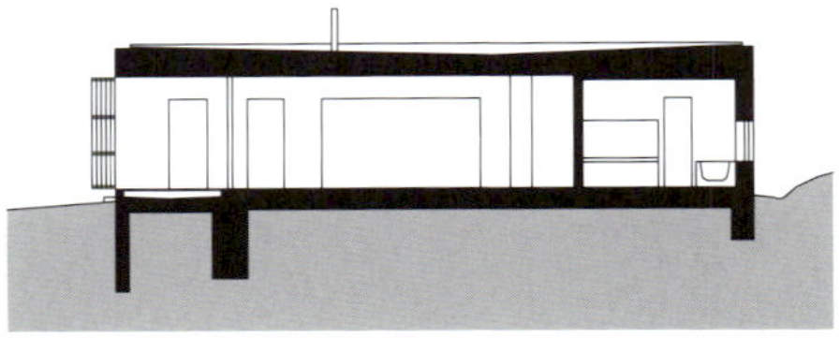

Hvozdná u Zlína / Studio Olgoj Chorchoj

Authors: D. Paterko, M. Froněk, J. Němeček, K. Hroncová / www.olgojchorchoj.cz
Design and construction process: 2007 – 2011 | Plot size: 2,852 m^2 | Building footprint: 432 m^2
Photos: Kristina Hrabětová

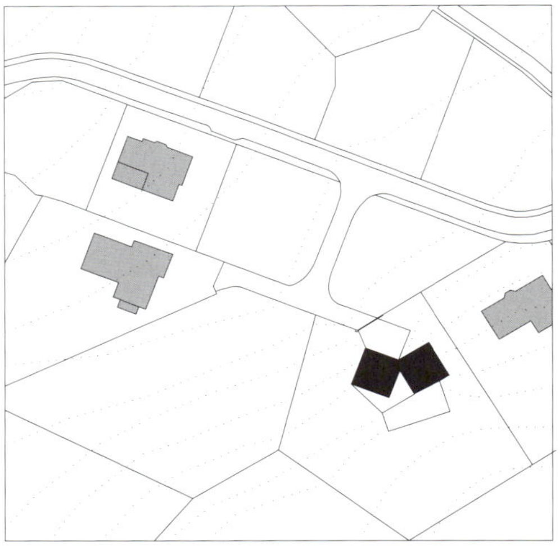

The building consists of two crystal-shaped volumes, turned towards each other and aligned with the property lines, with the roof and walls clad in a uniform material. One wing is two storeys high while the other has three levels, thus defining each section's different form. Access to the property from the road is at the building's basement level. At the height of the living areas (the second aboveground floor), a third wing with a grass-covered walk-on roof and housing a swimming pool is partly sunken into the slope. Together, the three sections form an atrium facing the woods to the south that provides ample privacy while visually connecting the interior spaces. The third floor housing the master bedroom faces to the east and provides access to the pool roof. The load-bearing structure consists of cast-in-situ reinforced concrete walls, steel pillars in the more open sections, and the partial use of hydrotechnical concrete.

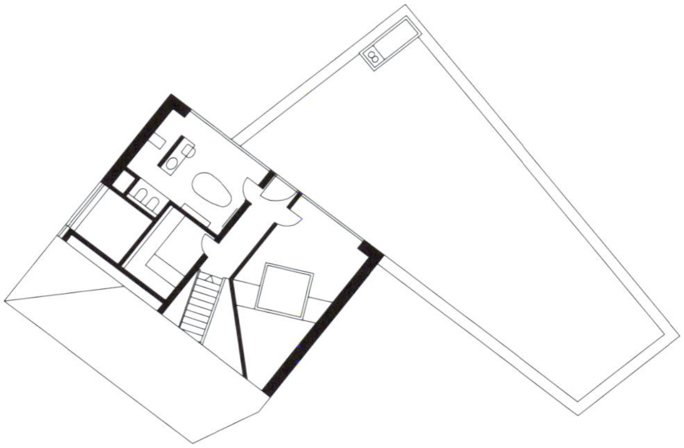

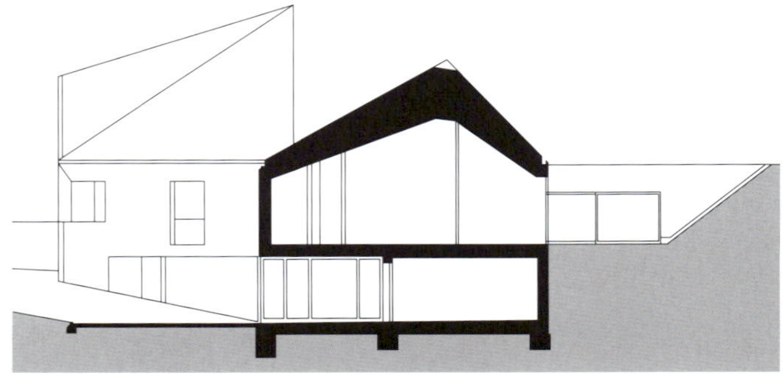

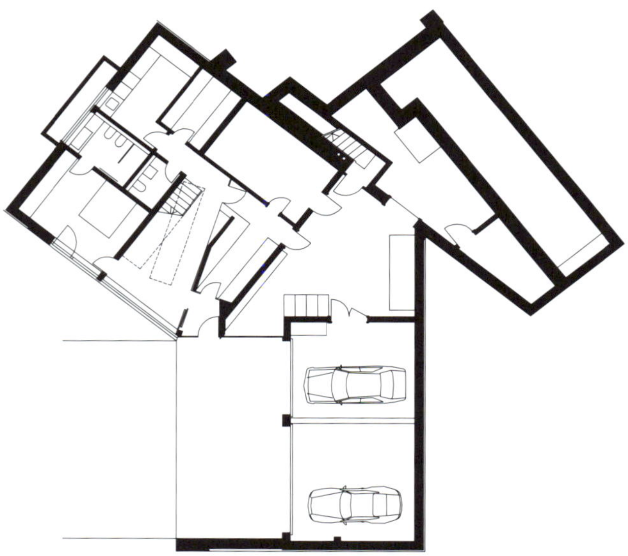

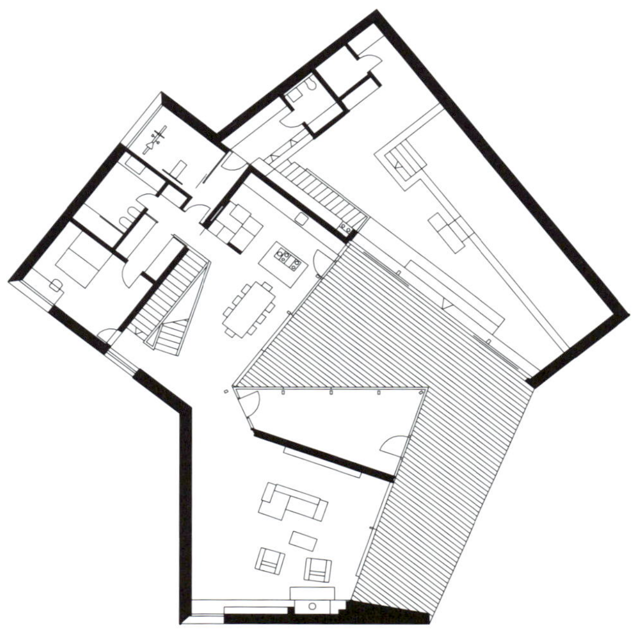

Pernink / FAM Architects

Authors: Pavel Nasadil / www.famarchitekti.cz /

Design and construction process: 2007 – 2011 | Plot size: 680 m² | Building footprint: 66 m²

Photos: Tomáš Balej

The house is located 820 meters above sea level in the village of Pernink in a valley carved by a wild stream. It is oriented with its narrower side facing into the prevailing western winds. The house is a hybrid of a small residential retreat and a guesthouse, with facilities for skiing and nature hiking. Its form is largely defined by the local topography, with its orientation providing views of the surrounding woodland landscape. The main load-bearing walls are made of 490mm-thick super-insulated blocks. As we move from the entrance to the living room on the upper floor, we twice pass through this mass, which thus lends a sense of intimacy and protection against the elements. The various indoor ceiling heights are reflected in the exterior building form.

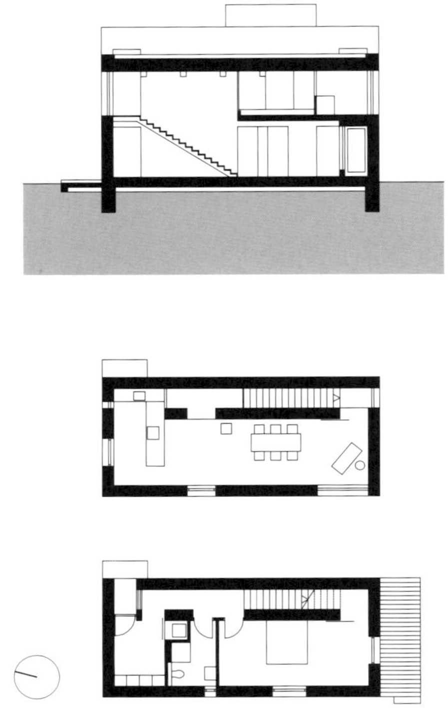

Buš / Markéta Cajthamlová

Authors: Markéta Cajthamlová, Jan Krejčí / www.arch.cz/cajthamlova /
Design and construction process. 2007 – 2011 Plot size: 2,992 m² | Building footprint: 210 m²
Photos: Ester Havlová

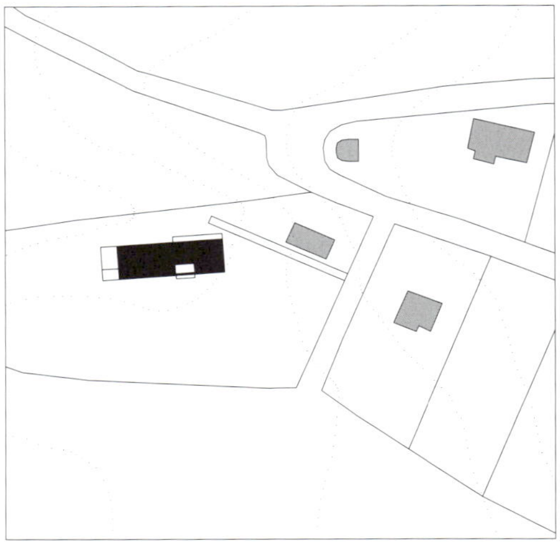

Located on a mildly sloping site on the edge of a village, the building provides a sense of connection to nature without being disturbed by the surrounding houses. The site is surrounded by mature greenery. The building layout consists of a main living space with a kitchen and living room, two bedrooms, a bathroom with a sauna and steam room, a toilet, and a storage room. The main living room opens onto a covered south-facing terrace with a whirlpool and natural pool. The load-bearing walls are made of dry-stacked concrete blocks and are insulated using mineral wool. The facade is made of cedar-wood cladding mounted on a timber frame. The wooden ceilings are made of joint beams, and the roof is a green roof system. Cedar is also used in the ceilings and as a framing material for the windows. The house is heated using an air/water heat pump. Heat distribution is via a combination of underfloor heating, radiators and in-floor convectors.

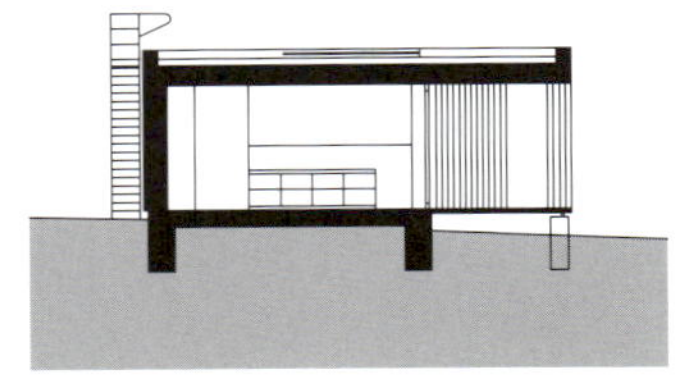

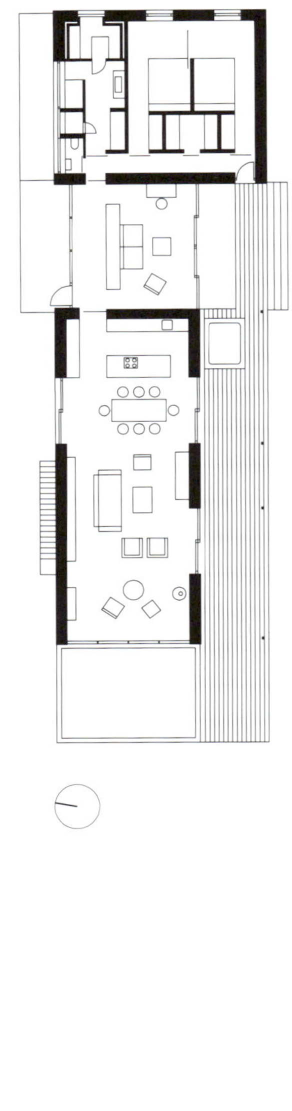

Roudnice nad Labem / Ivan Kroupa

Author: Ivan Kroupa / www.ivankroupa.cz /
Design and construction process: 2008 – 2011 | Plot size: 2,610 m² | Building footprint: 412.5 m²
Photos: Jan Kuděj, Ivan Kroupa

The family house is integrated into a promontory above town. Rising from the terrain, its serene concrete walls have been left to be gradually overgrown by vegetation, slowly becoming a part of the terrain itself. The large glass facade and terrace wing provide a connection between interior and exterior. Inside, the design continues the approach of incorporating the building into the landscape: the sandy surfaces on the floors, ceilings and walls merge with the pool to create a kind of indoor beach with a raw sandy finish. In the living areas and in the double-height library, the surfaces switch to a smooth white finish. Later changes to the garden do not fit the architectural design nor do they promote the building's integration into the landscape beneath Říp Mountain. With time, however, the artificial landscape of the green areas may return to the natural surroundings.

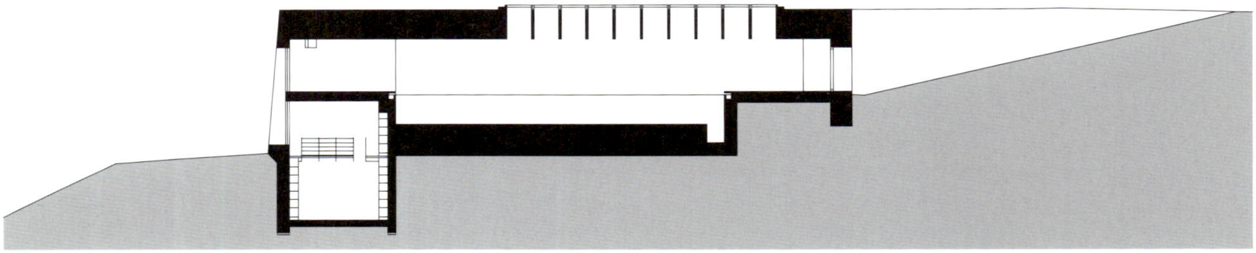

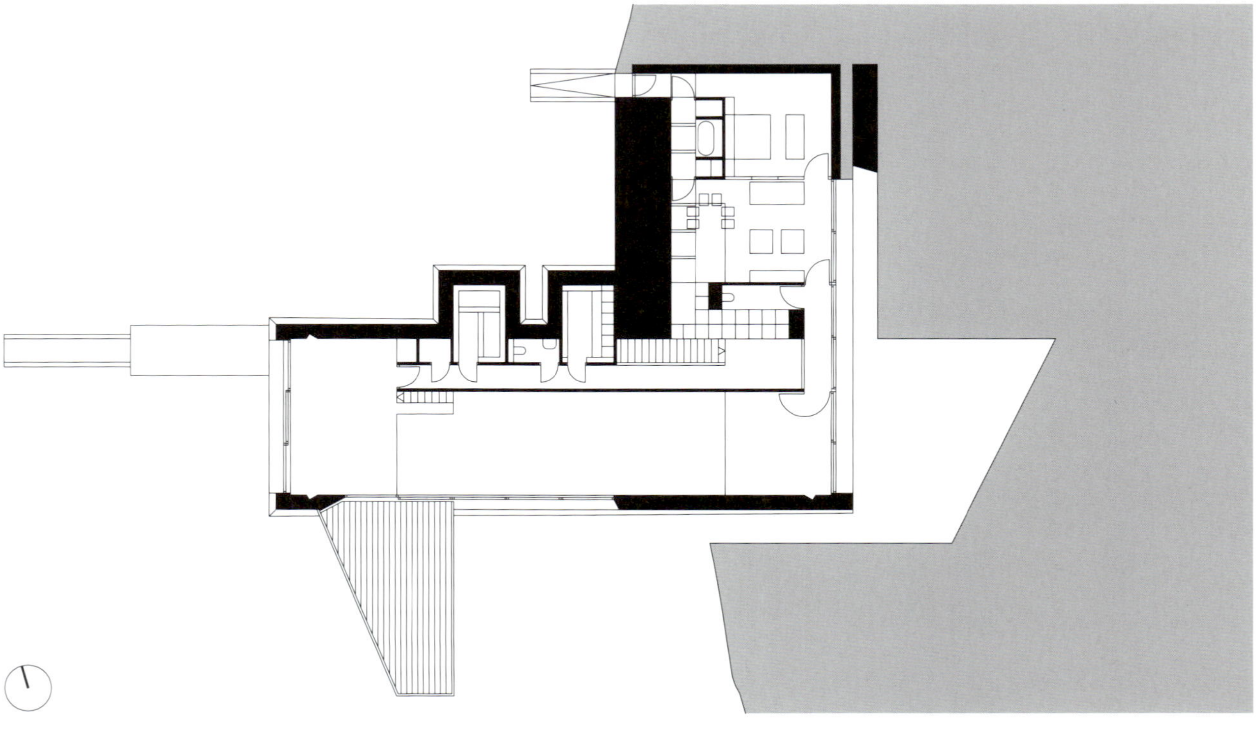

Prague-Lochkov / D3A

Authors: Jaroslav Zima, Milan Bulva, Sabina Měšťanová / www.d3a.cz /
Design and construction process: 2008 – 2012 | Plot size: 630 m² | Building footprint: 272 m²
Photos: Filip Šlapal

The building is located among older existing housing on a triangular site with a high difference in elevation. In terms of layout, it is divided into two connected parts. Abutting the street is a garage with entrance and hallway. The building's main twin-story mass opens up to the courtyard via a glass facade, thus making the intimate courtyard a part of the large living space with kitchen. The utility rooms have been placed into the hillside. On the upper floor are three rooms and a hallway with a wardrobe wall illuminated by a roof light. The two smaller rooms and bathroom open directly onto the terrace. The building, including facades and roof, is made of reinforced concrete. The facades can be covered by louvers. Heating is provided by a heat pump. The artworks are by Petr Písařík.

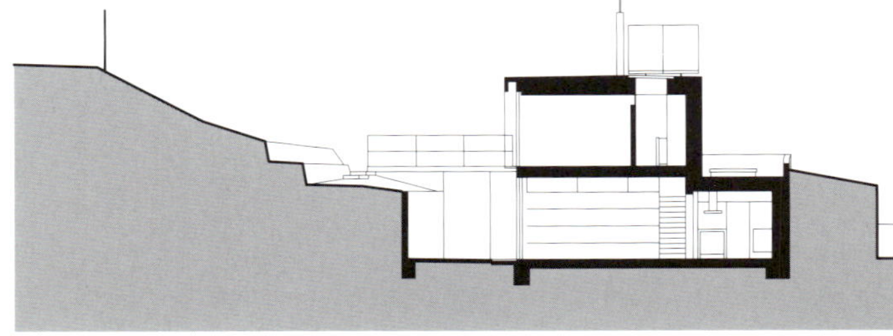

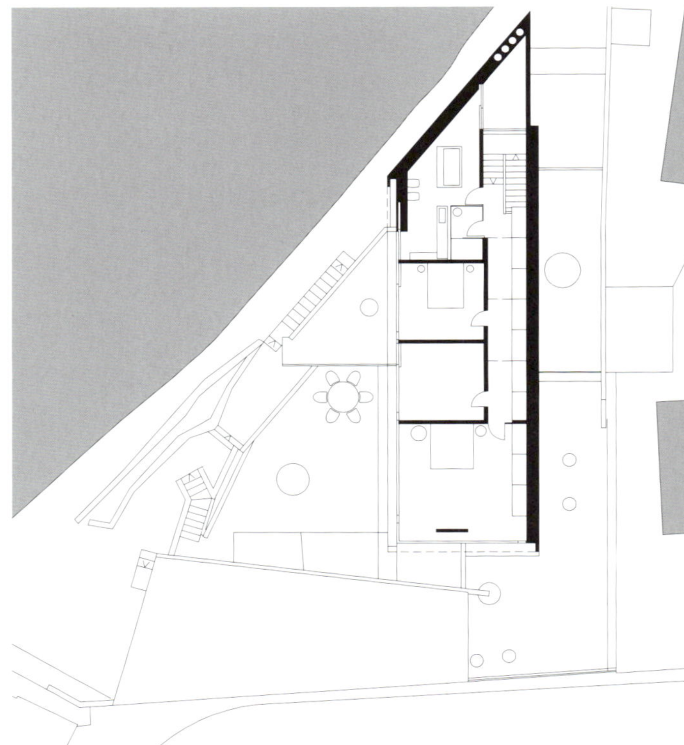

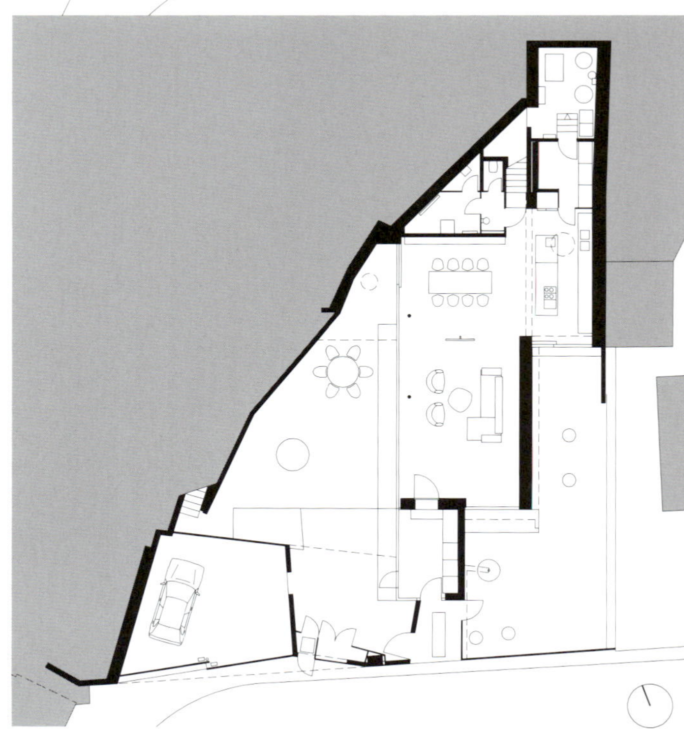

Jevany / Architektura

Author: David Kraus / www.archi.cz /

Design and construction process: 2009 – 2011 | Plot size: 3,696 m² | Building footprint: 391 m²

Photos: Filip Šlapal

This single-floor low energy blockwork house was built on a wooded site near a lake in Jevany, where the water surface creates a constantly changing scenery. The building's lake-facing side is glazed, the rear side is closed, and there are also windows facing east and west. In terms of layout, it is divided into three levels. The rear wing is for utility rooms, while the front contains the living spaces. These all face south, and also receive additional light from the east and west thanks to the windows on those sides. The building is divided into three zones: one for adults, one for children and one for common areas such as the living room. The facade is made of natural stone; the roof and ceiling are made of exposed concrete. The floors in the bathrooms are made of white screed; the walls are clad in marble. Stone is used in the living room to form a wall for the fireplace and kitchen. Heating is via a heat pump with underfloor heating.

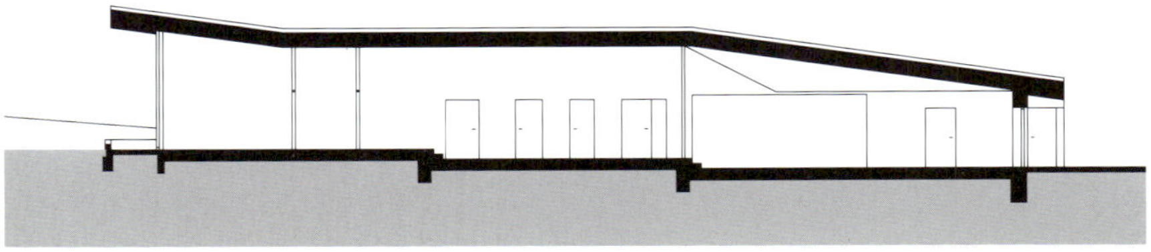

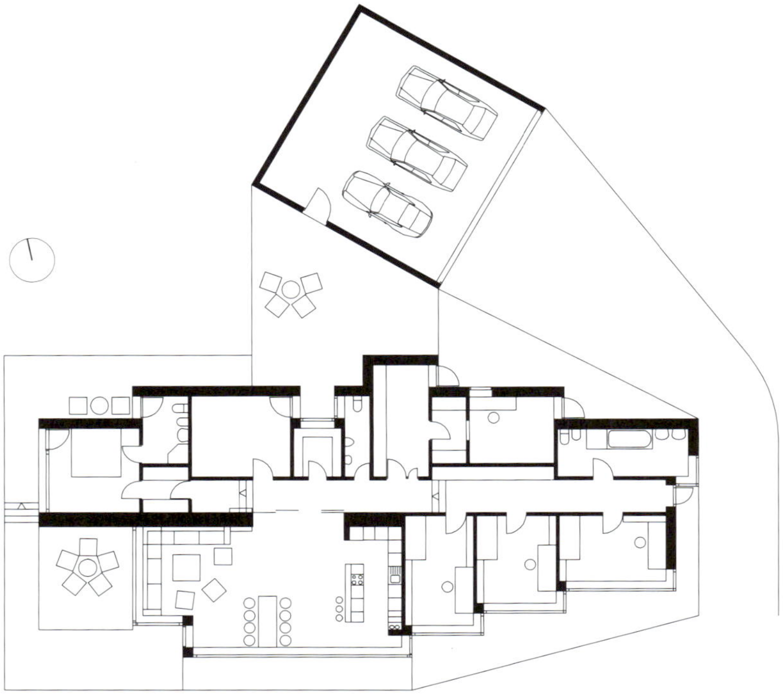

Český ráj / stempel & tesar

Authors: Ján Stempel, Jan Jakub Tesař / www.stempel-tesar.com /
Design and construction process: 2009 – 2012 | Plot size: 2,715 m² | Building footprint: 189 m²
Photos: FOTES

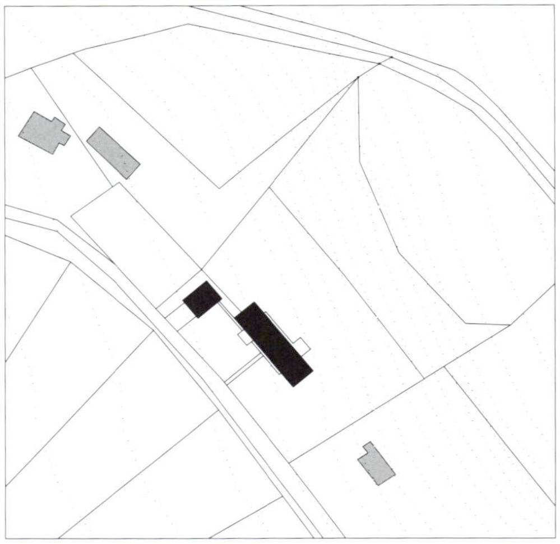

This double-family house is located in the level 2 natural protection zone of the Český Ráj Nature Reserve. The design is inspired by the principles of local vernacular architecture – half of the building is built in stone and half in wood, thus defining its division into a working area and a living area. Another source of inspiration came from drive-through barns, whose design was reflected in the large glazed areas that bring southern light into the interior while preserving the unique northern views of the forest and the peaks of the Giant Mountains. The airy interior reflects the building's exterior. The primary material is wood, combined with colorful inbuilt furniture. The simple form and combination of natural materials make the house feel like a country home despite its contemporary look. Although large in volume, the building appears compact thanks to its physical arrangement.

Vaňov / 3+1 architekti

Authors: Pavel Plánička, Matěj Páral, Bruno Panenka / www.31architekti.cz /
Design and construction process: 2009 – 2012 | Plot size: 980 m^2 | Building footprint: 113 m^2
Photos : Pavel Plánička

The building's design responds to the client's personal ties to the site and the panoramic views of the valley below, while also taking into account the somewhat poorly oriented and steeply sloping site. In many ways (position, materials) the new building respects the original cottage on the plot, and was also inspired by its form (single pitched roof, covered terrace etc.). The house was designed as a lightweight timber-framed building using linear foundations tied to the base slab. Construction involved the use of 625mm modules in the horizontal as well as vertical direction, with the proportions determined by the size of the timber frame module. The color scheme was inspired by the adjoining garden.

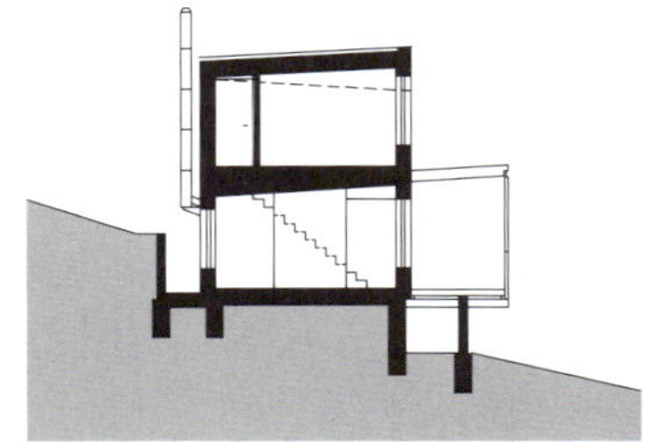

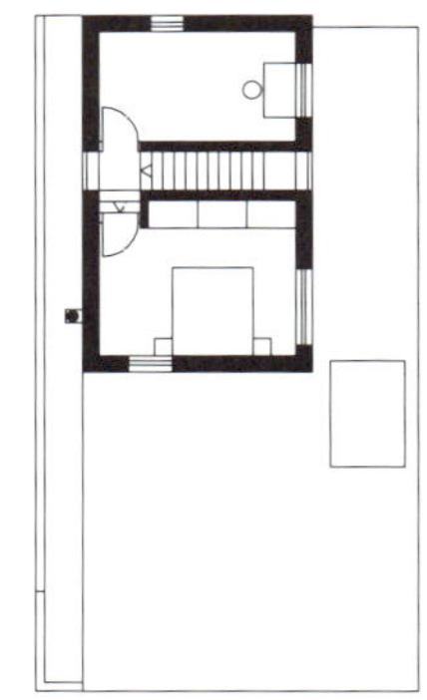

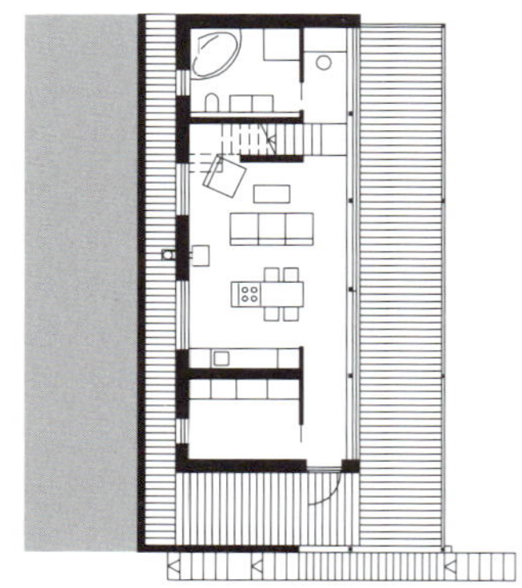

Stará Role / A69 - architekti

Authors: B. Redčenkov, P. Tomášek, J. Wertig, V. Danda, P. Jahelka, J. Macáková / www.a69.cz / Design and construction process: 2009 – 2014 | Plot size: 1,177 m² | Building footprint: 570 m²

Photos: Tomáš Rasl

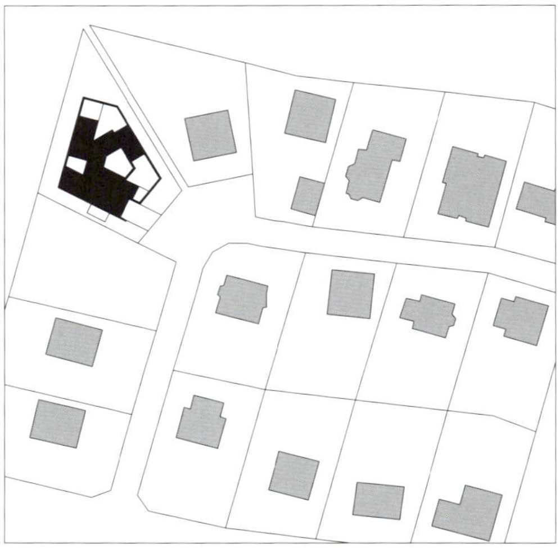

The project makes 100% use of the plot. Instead of a house with a garden, the architects have designed a never-ending series of motifs with a house. The building takes up the entire area, erasing transitions between indoor and outdoor and vice versa. The design was based primarily on a typological diagram that considered each room's requirements for level of intimacy, sunlight, neighborhood interaction, and size. This diagram eventually took shape as a spiral. Spaces with greater requirements for intimacy are located higher up and closer to the middle of the plot. The spiral begins by the technical facilities near the entrance and culminates at the master bedroom. The surfaces have a soft texture and an almost monochromatic coloring.

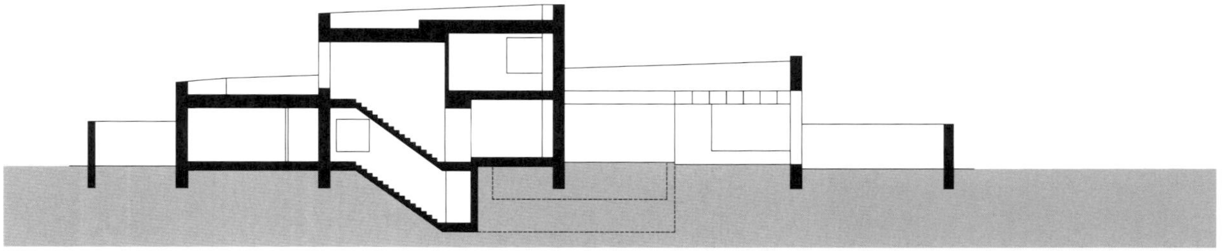

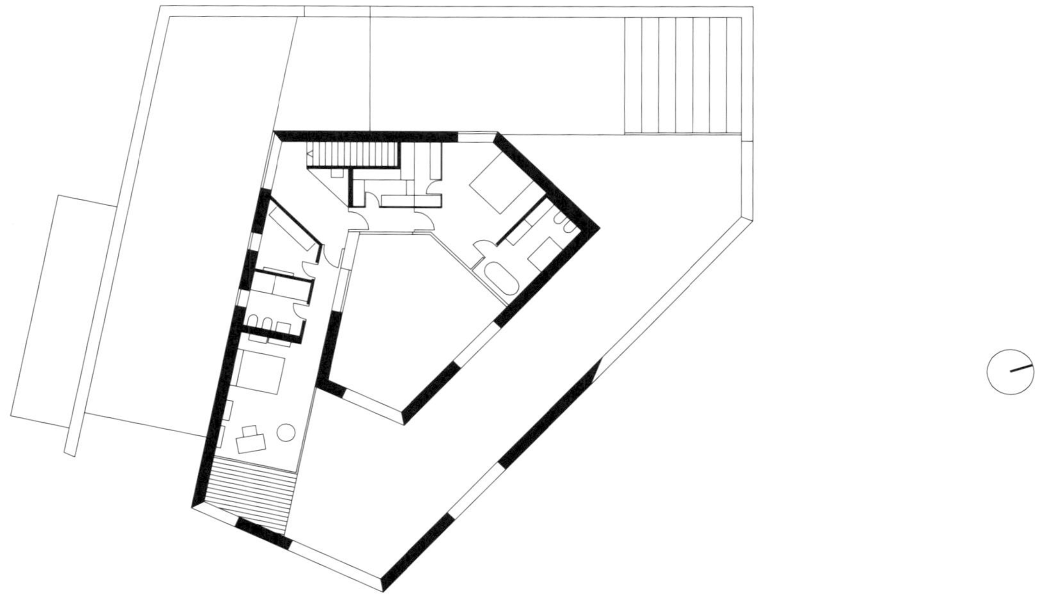

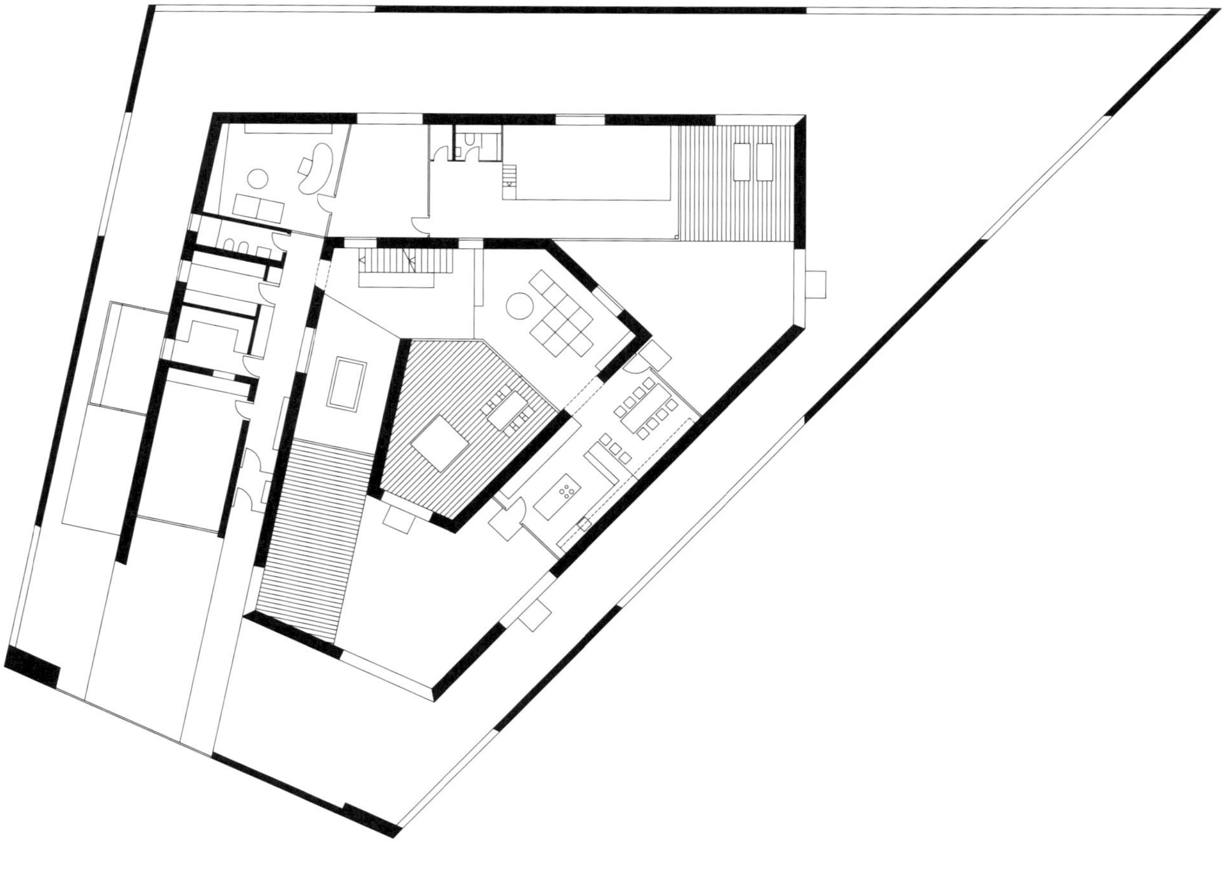

Mníšek / KSA

Authors: David Kopecký, Pavel Mejtský, Ján Studený / www.ksastudeny.sk /
Design and construction process: 2010 – 2011 | Plot size: 1,931 m² | Building footprint: 300 m²
Photos: Ondřej Kocourek, Kristina Hrabětová

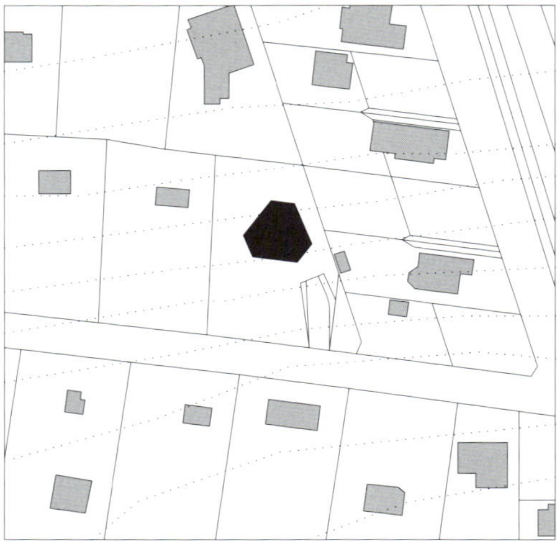

From the street, the building feels a little like a bunker or dugout – small and self-enclosed. The interior design, however, makes exactly the opposite impression. The hexagonal building opens up to the garden through large glass walls with sliding doors. The interior is very austere, with the main role played by the sliding partitions and doors. Structurally, the house is made of poured concrete, with the load-bearing outer walls supporting a ceiling spanning 18 meters, which is further held up by the inner core that houses the bathrooms. The hexagonal concrete shell roof, ground wave, and simple organic form allow for the full exploitation of flat slab elements. The building integrates the most progressive passive and active systems for optimum energy savings and a stable indoor climate, further supported by the use of a green roof that blends in with the garden surrounding the house.

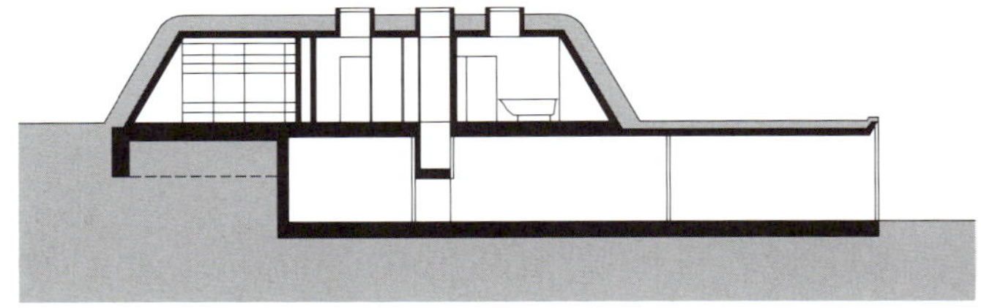

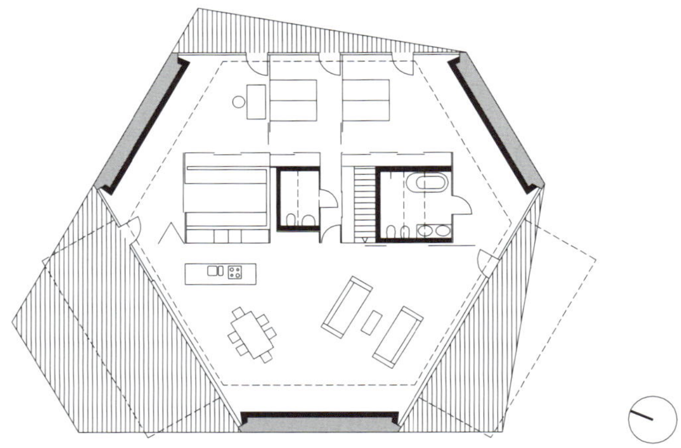

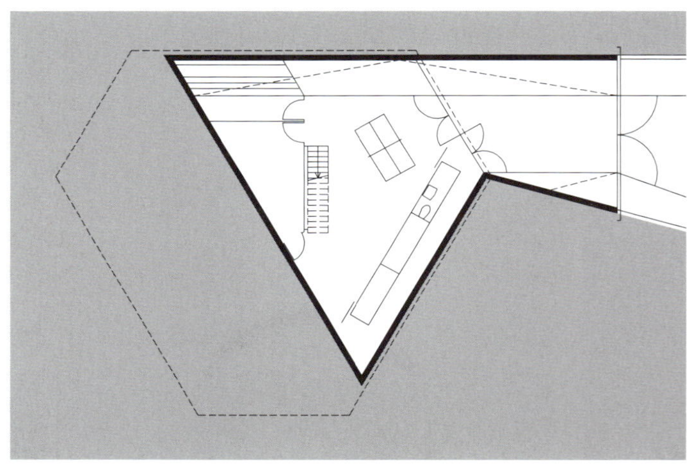

Zbečno / A.LT architekti

Authors: Peter Lacko, Filip Tittelbach, Michal Šiška / www.a-LT.cz /

Design and construction process: 2010 – 2011 | Plot size: 1,640 m² | Building footprint: 50 m²

Photos: Tomáš Rasl

This minimal family house was created on the site of a non-functional 1950s holiday cabin. The building is located in a nature conservation area where new construction is forbidden. As a result, the design had to limit itself to the renovation of the existing building. The original garage was converted into a utility room. Because of the steeply sloping terrain, the new building stands on wooden stilts. The hexagonal layout provides for a west-facing orientation towards the sun and enables views in all directions. The living room is situated downstairs next to the kitchen and bathroom. Two bedrooms, an office and another bathroom are located upstairs. The building is made entirely of wood using large wooden KLH panels; it is insulated from the outside and clad in larch panels.

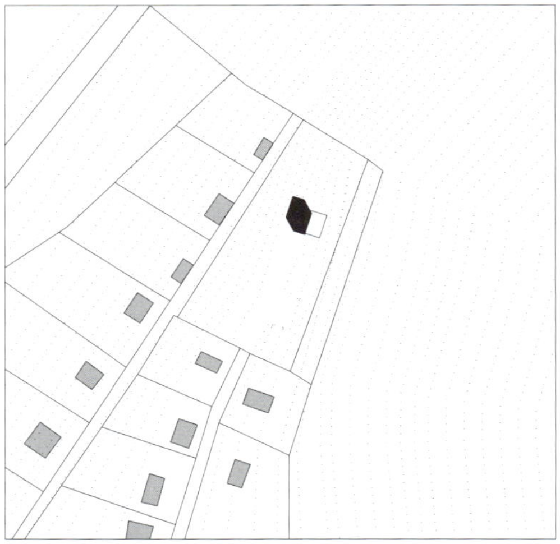

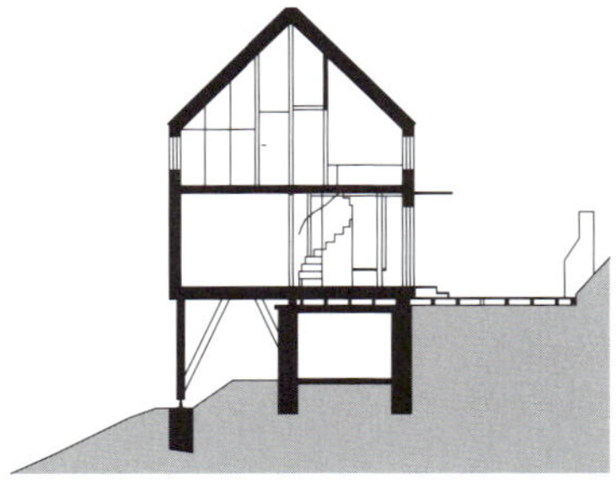

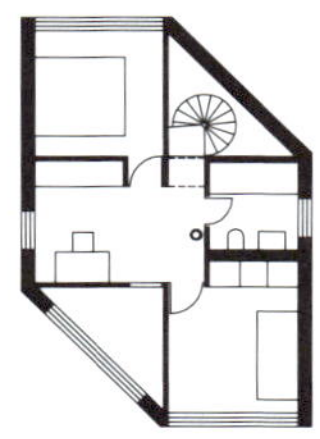

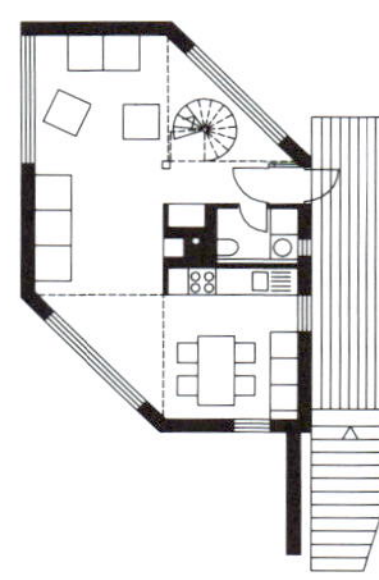

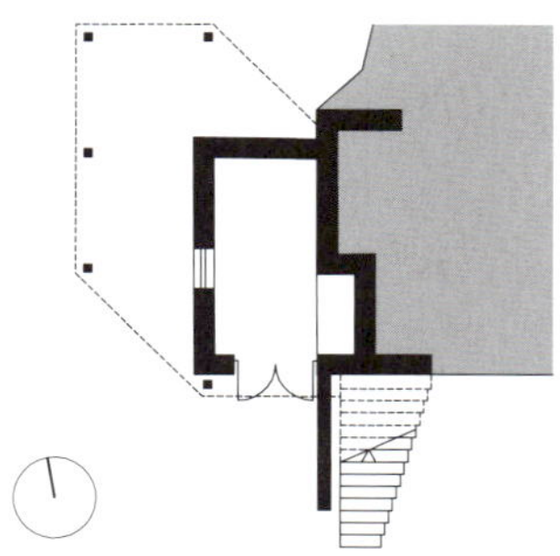

Frýdava / Uhlík architekti

Authors: Petr Uhlík, Zuzana Šuleková / www.uhlikarchitekti.cz /
Design and construction process: 2010 – 2013 | Plot size: 2,500 m² | Building footprint: 106 m²
Photos: Tomáš Balej

The house is located high above sea level (745 meters) on a steep slope by the Lipno Reservoir with an unfavorable northeast orientation. Its design reflects an attempt at resolving these difficult conditions. The building is divided into two sections. The lower concrete base contains bedrooms that are connected to the exterior by a terrace, plus a small wellness room and technical room in the basement. Resting on top of this base is a large rectangular section with a glass facade; it projects out eight meters on both sides, thus seeming to levitate among the trees over the lake. The open, sun-filled living space offers panoramic views of the lake thanks to a glass facade that can be regulated or even closed completely using folding shutters. The foundation is made of reinforced concrete sandwich panels, and the upper rectangular section is made of a steel truss frame clad in fire-resistant HPL compact laminate boards.

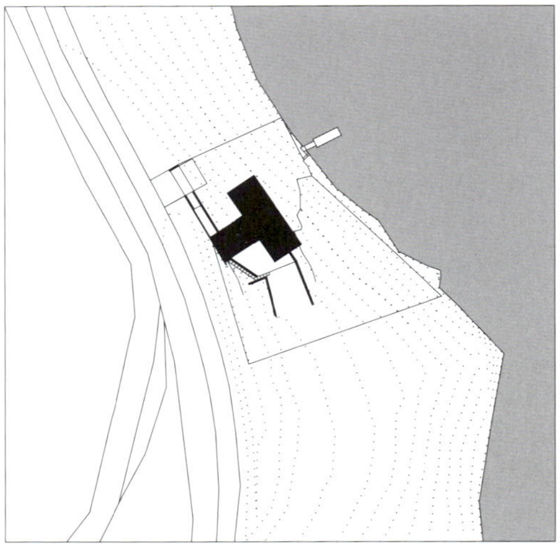

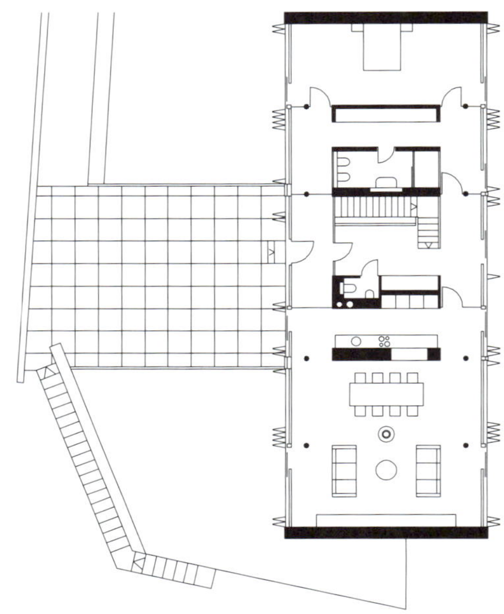

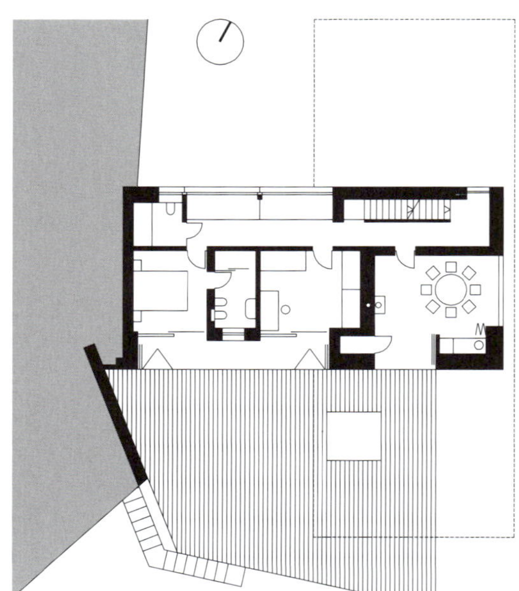

Litomyšl / AP atelier

Authors: Josef Pleskot, Norbert Schmidt, Jiří Trčka / www.arch.cz/pleskot /
Design and construction process: 2010 – 2014 | Plot size: 1,931 m² | Building footprint: 523 m²
Photos: Tomáš Souček

As per the client's request, this family house located in an architecturally diverse neighborhood on the northern edge of the town of Litomyšl was built as a single-level building centered around a central atrium. All living spaces are accessible from this unroofed central "living room". The outer facades transition into property walls to form a kind of hard shell protecting life inside from the surrounding world. By comparison, on the inside the house feels soft and open, with the large glass surfaces and numerous doors providing visual as well as physical connections. This linkage between the interior and exterior is further accentuated by the roofed terrace framing three sides of the atrium. The fourth side of this "living-room courtyard" features a garden and small pond whose changes with the seasons are an integral part of life inside the house.

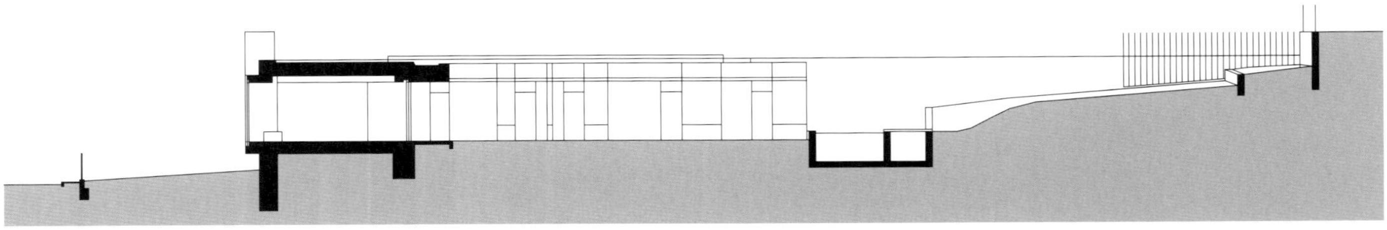

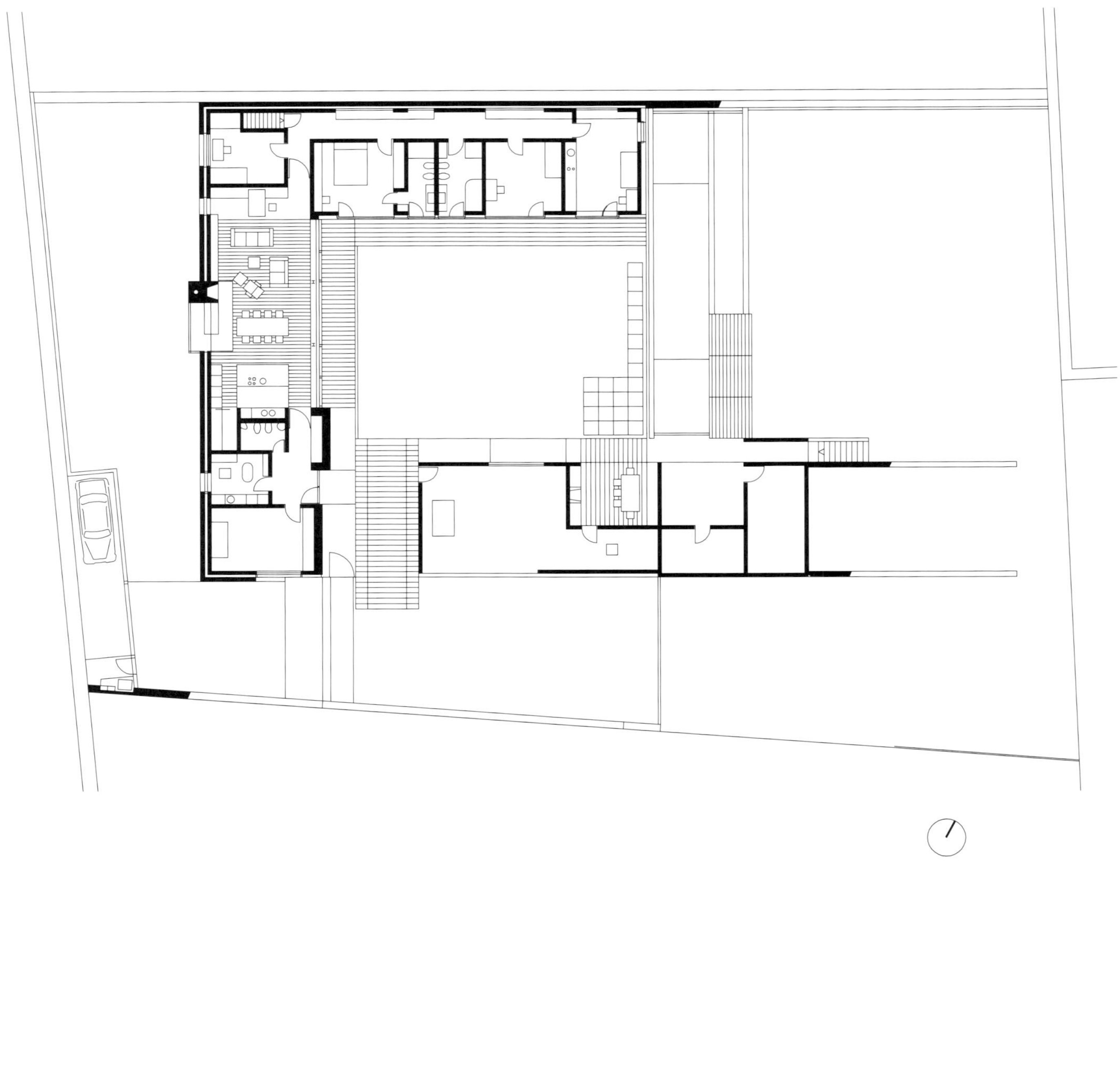

Prague / Schindler Seko Architects

Author: Jan Schindler / www.schindlerseko.cz /
Design and construction process: 2011 – 2013 | Plot size: 228 m^2 | Building footprint: 136 m^2
Photos : Ondřej Polák

The building is located within the existing built-up area of the former village of Tejnka near the Prague Castle district. The architectural design involved the new construction of a homogenous three-story poured concrete structure (including new foundations), inserted into existing historic walls, plus an annex building and raised inhabitable attic space. The basic volumetric composition consists of two elements: the restored historic facades and the new annex located along the plot's southern border. The latter, a compact object made of poured architectural concrete with a flat roof at the level of the adjacent street, provides a space for parking and for entering the house. In the old building, too, the walls, ceilings and staircases were made using poured concrete. All surfaces are treated with formwork made of natural timber boards. The floors are made of machine-smoothed industrial concrete slab.

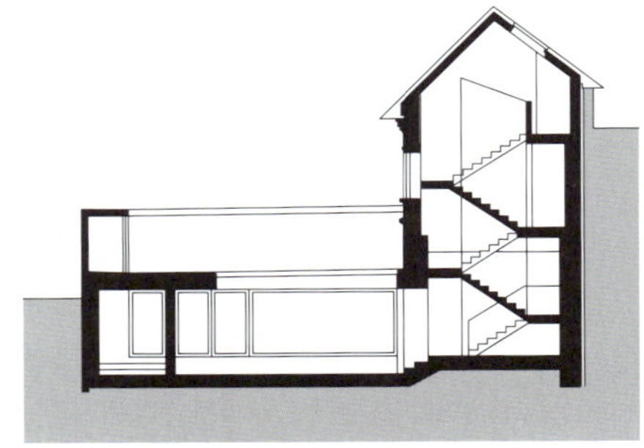

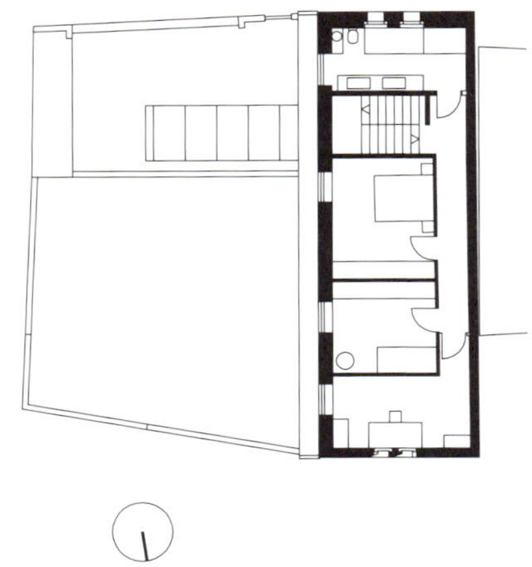

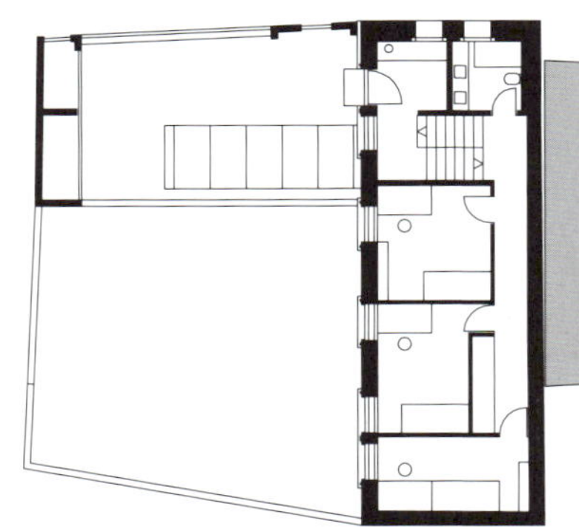

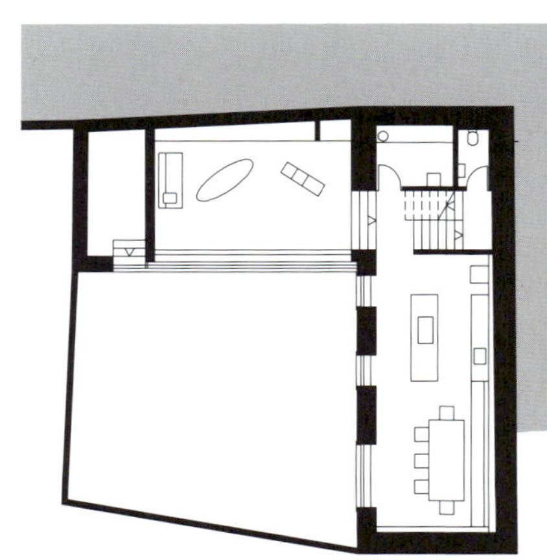

The Contemporary Czech House

Eugene Asse
Architect, Professor, Dean of MARCH School of Architecture in Moscow

To my shame, I never managed to visit the Czech Republic until this year, despite the fact that my connection with the country, its culture and my colleagues has been ongoing for decades. However, I agreed to write this brief introduction only after I visited the country and saw modern Czech architecture in person.

On the one hand it is true that foreigners like me have no idea of the scale of the phenomena (e.g., how many architect-designed private houses have been built in the Czech Republic), or of the stylistic and conceptual diversity of Czech architecture. As a result, one might suspect that the compiler of this album has made his choices simply according to his own tastes, and that there are only thirty-three houses in the whole country worth publishing (in Russia one could assemble an album of fifty good houses, but they would truly be the exception to the enormous mass of terrible housing construction). On the other hand, if I had not been told in advance that the album was dedicated to Czech houses, I might have thought that it is a pan-European collection – so impeccably embedded within the international professional context are the collected projects. A careful study of the pictures and drawings shows that the social context in which these buildings exist is generally European, too. Having finally visited the Czech Republic, I can assure the reader that the projects collected here are no accident, but that they reflect general trends in modern Czech architecture as well as in social practice.

Thumbing through the pages of this book, one clearly understands that the contemporary Czech house is integrated confidently into the global architectural and civilizational context – the thirty-three houses selected for this book reflect almost all the main international design trends for private houses. From this perspective, I find the selection nearly flawless. Here we can speak not just of individual projects, but of a single phenomenon that can be called the "Contemporary Czech House."

What is a contemporary Czech house? It is relatively small in size, relatively inexpensive, but not poor. Plots are also small in size and not intended for agricultural use. The Czech house is home to a fairly prosperous and educated family, with liberal values, good taste and a preference for the latest high-quality architecture and design. Women in these houses are emancipated, and children are free to explore all its spaces. The house is clean and empty. Of course, the lack of visible traces of the tenants' lives in the houses is most likely due to the strict rules of architectural photography.

The contemporary Czech house shows the neo-modernist rigor of geometry, minimalist simplicity and modesty, elegance, and attention to detail. It brings to mind the aristocratic origins of modern Czech architecture, dating back to Mies van der Rohe and Adolf Loos.

The Czech house features mostly white walls, wooden floors, large windows and glass walls, exposed design, natural materials (wood, metal, concrete), a double-height living room, an open kitchen, and a combination of polished and brutal surfaces. It is clear that life in this house is as simple and transparent as its interior.

The surprising similarity between the Czech word "dům" (house) and the Russian word "duma" ("thought"), reminds us Heidegger's assertion of a common root for the words Bauen, Wohnen, Denken and the triune of the concepts of build, live and think. From this point of view, we can say that the Czech house is inhabited by thought. Thought makes the house clear and precise. At the same time, the abundance of space, the movement of light, and the collision of materials fill the Czech house with poetry. Recall that Heidegger liked to quote Hölderlin: "poetically man dwells".

I think that the balance between the rationality of common sense and the intuition of poetry, between mind and soul, is the most precious quality and foundation of Architecture as an art.

I find this quality present in the "Contemporary Czech House."

Opulent Austerity

Ákos Moravánszky

Titular Professor for the Theory of Architecture at the Institute for the History and Theory of Architecture, ETH Zurich

In its matter-of-factness, the title *Czech Houses* may sound like an understatement, but in reality it promises more than just a collection of residential buildings from the Czech Republic. It suggests something more specific: Czech houses as a species of its own kind, even as a program. The notion of Czech Houses claims, rightly or wrongly, a certain consensus regarding what constitutes architectural quality – at least with regard to the architecture of the single-family house. This latter qualification is important, since it implies that while the architecture of the city might follow international trends, the family house in its natural surroundings follows its own rules, because it is closer to nature, to the region, and first of all, to the country – to its materials and its specific tradition. This is what I mean by Czech Houses as program.

We have to ask, however, whether this distinction between city and country can still be maintained. In other words, did the spaces that we describe as the "countryside", as "natural" or "rural", really escape the process of modernization and homogenization to serve as a basis for a "rooted" architecture? And if such spaces do indeed exist, are they necessarily private? The family home as the site of resistance against global urbanization?

Certainly, the family house has been a testing ground for new ideas almost in every European country. But it is Prague and Brno, where the most opulent examples of the modern home have been realized – Adolf Loos's Villa Müller in Prague and Mies van der Rohe's Villa Tugendhat in Brno, to name just two of the most famous. Notably, both houses were built for clients who lived with their servants, maids and chauffeurs, like the grand bourgeoisie of the 19th century. If the social agenda of the modern movement had to give way to the wishes of the private client, its austere aesthetic was easy to reconcile with exuberant materiality.

If we look at architectural books published in the Czech Republic, we find that the architecture of residential buildings occupies a singular position. Many recent books and even book series have been dedicated to single-family houses built in various regions and cities of the country. These books offer selections of outstanding buildings, mostly from the 20th century. This a truly unique phenomenon when compared to architectural publications in other countries, where the detached house is found either in books for designers (who present new typologies or constructional details) or in picture books for home-builders searching for ideas ranging from the Caribbean style to minimalism. But these Czech books on residential architecture lack the somewhat voyeuristic character of such popular publications, and are not afraid to show grainy archival photographs. Indeed, Czech residential architecture developed certain physiognomic peculiarities from early on. Browsing through the pages of the leading architectural journal of the Austro-Hungarian Monarchy, *Der Architekt*, we find that one distinguishing feature is a certain lighter touch, embracing Art Nouveau with a playfulness and "artistry" that is closer to Paris than to Vienna. Almost as a shadow of this playfulness, however, we also recognize a more sober, dry, even rough strain that can be described as austerity. The use of brick, a material largely absent from residential architecture elsewhere in Central Europe because of its industrial associations, characterizes some of the most outstanding early modern houses in Bohemia. Since the clients were frequently industrialists engaged in building the country's infrastructure, they had no reservations at all regarding the use of brick or iron.

The architects who designed the Czech houses in this book are certainly aware of the great achievements of Czech modernism, but their direct experience ties them to the drab materiality of real socialism, prefab concrete, crammed apartments and jerry-built weekend cottages. The new situation after the fall of socialism can be therefore best described as a veritable "spatial turn": a growing intellectual (and financial) "investment" in space rather than in the veneers or cladding necessary to cover the rudimentary construction. This "spatial turn" does not necessarily mean more cubic meters, but rather innovative typologies and the avoidance of decorative details, which had been abundant in late socialist postmodernism. Since the austere form has no aesthetic value in itself, the question is how to turn this program into an aesthetic – into a form that is as recognizable and concise as the houses of Adolf Loos.

Another significant aspect of this architecture is its materiality, which is very different from the functionalist villas of the twenties and thirties with their white stucco facades. In this respect, the buildings in this book offer a wide range of materials – wood, stone, steel or concrete, frequently in combination with soil or greenery. This tension between mimicry and contrast to the environment shows the awkward relationship with nature. Nature today is always transformed, shaped, landscaped and urbanized. In some cases, the surfaces of the houses are treated as "naturalized" fragments, and the spaces are excavated or covered with earth and foliage. The dream of the private house as escape, as reconciliation with nature, must remain a dream; and urban reality is not as absent as some of the photographs may want us to believe.

The uniqueness, the exceptional character of the works presented here has less to do with the regionalist or national claim that the title makes than with today's historic moment, when a generation of architects socialized and educated under one political system is now working under entirely different circumstances. Combined with a self-imposed restriction, this experience of dramatically expanded possibilities results in the celebration of textural effects and a technical precision that was hitherto unattainable. The pathos of this opulent austerity lies in the re-working and modification of the modernist ethos, extending and enriching it with new sensory qualities and material, technical and spatial possibilities.

Adolf Loos, Villa Müller in Prague — Photo: Martin Polák

Ludwig Mies van der Rohe, Villa Tugendhat in Brno — Photo: David Židlický

The Good Results of Patient People

Adam Gebrian

Architect, theorist and promoter of architecture; lecturer at the Architectural Institute in Prague

The quality of Czech architecture has been continually increasing in the 25 years since the fall of the communist regime. Slowly, but surely. This can be perhaps best seen when we look at family houses – maybe because it is a field that requires close cooperation between client and architect. The client is usually a private individual, and in most cases he is investing his own money in a house where he intends to spend the rest of his life. This means that he cares a lot about the final result. Great architecture thus does not arise only by a client giving the architect unlimited freedom during the design process and letting him do what he wants – although most people still think this is how it works. On the contrary: It regularly arises from a close dialogue between client and architect, from an interaction that usually takes place over quite a long time. The houses presented in this book are the outcome of a processes whose long-term nature is the reason we do not see more similar examples. If you want something unusual, what you really need to be prepared for is not so much that it will be expensive but that it will take a long time.

The book includes several examples that took more than five – and, in some cases, nearly ten – years from first idea to full completion. What you see here is thus the work of very patient people.

In *Modern Architecture, A Critical History*, Kenneth Frampton writes that we can find "very different levels of general architectural maturity in otherwise equally advanced nations, and surprisingly sophisticated manifestations of tectonic creativity in countries that might otherwise be regarded as underdeveloped."[1]

The Czech Republic (and formerly Czechoslovakia) is not a country whose architecture has attracted international attention. There are many reasons for this. One is a lack of architects of global significance through whom it might be possible to broadcast the quality of our country's architecture to the world. This is how it was in the past, this is how it is now, and this is probably how it will be in the near future. But it does not automatically mean that it is all wrong.

In recent years, architect Ján Stempel has published two books that, taken together, present 176 individually designed houses. This publication includes a selection of 33, which still show a wide range of possible approaches to the individual needs of individual builders. We find large houses and (the majority) small houses; low, high, narrow, or long houses; new projects and renovations; houses in the countryside, in dense urban centers and in suburbia; on flat property or on a slope; made from concrete, wood, bricks or steel; modern, abstract, or traditional with a gable roof; distinctive, subtle or introverted. Despite this diversity of possible approaches, we can still identify an overall attitude of restraint and moderation. This is partially determined by national tradition and further supported by the architect and the editor – the selection thus reveals his values. This book contains not a single building that might have a detrimental impact on the environment for either neighbors or passers-by.

The existence of many different responses to different environments is very good news. I have long been convinced that the level of Czech architects is very good, and that it results from the quality of the schools, which can hold their own in an international comparison. The overall level of taste in the democratic conditions of just one quarter of a century is a different story. If we look at the recent past, we can see that we have significantly improved when it comes to activities that we engage in on a regular basis. We buy quality and timeless clothes and shoes; we are more concerned about what we eat. But things are much worse when it comes to the design and construction of new homes. Few people have multiple experiences building a house (although this book does include some examples). It is no accident that one of the architects presented in the book, Stanislav Fiala, says that the best client is the one who has built at least two poorly designed houses and doesn't want to make the same mistake a third time.

The number of people interested in building a good family home does give hope that, after satisfying their private housing needs, they will focus on improving the environment in which they work or will become involved in their communities and thus influence the quality of publicly-financed buildings. The quality of public buildings is currently the biggest problem in the Czech Republic and one reason why Czech architecture remains invisible on the international level. We hope that this will change in the near future.

[1] Kenneth Frampton, Modern Architecture: A Critical History, Thames & Hudson, 1992, third edition, p. 328

With support from

This publication was supported by the Grant Agency of the Czech Technical University in Prague, grant no. SGS13/227/OHK1/3T/15

Special thanks to all homeowners, architects, contractors and photographers, whose help and kind support made this project possible.

Special thanks to Hana Tesařová and Lucie Vogelová

ČESKÉ DOMY

Ján Stempel
Jan Jakub Tesař
Ondřej Beneš

V oborech architektury a urbanismu představuje individuální bydlení, jakými jsou rodinné domy, vily, rezidence, rekreační objekty nebo usedlosti, významný segment. Z kvality a způsobu realizace - této jedné z nejstarších architektonických úloh - lze usuzovat na „stav společnosti". Bydlení představuje jednu ze základních potřeb člověka; to, co na první pohled působí zcela samozřejmě, je součástí proměn kultury a civilizačního vývoje a tím i možností, které otevírají nové stavební technologie. Mezi válkami byla architektura v Československu plnohodnotnou součástí nejprogresivnějšího architektonického dění – a takové výjimečné realizace jakými byly vila Tugendhat od Miese van der Rohe v Brně, Müllerova vila od Adolfa Loose v Praze, patří k uznávaným vrcholům světové architektury. Po roce 1948 s „vrchnostensky" prodiktovaným „socialistickým realismem" se tato vazba počíná ztrácet. S bruselským pavilonem (1958) a návratem k „autentické architektuře" se v šedesátých letech znovu pootevíraly cesty k mimořádným realizacím, vlnu vzestupu prožívala i výstavba rodinných domů. V následujících desítiletích, sedmdesátých i osmdesátých létech, zejména v létech tzv. normalizace, se do státem nepodporované individuální výstavby promítá ztráta perspektiv. Seberealizace, která byla často zmarněna ve vlastní profesi, nalézá vyjádření ve výstavbě rodinných domů „svépomocí" - v tomto kontextu šlo svým způsobem o „vnitřní emigraci". Zásadní zlom je spjat s rokem 1989. Končí centrálně plánované hospodářství s do značné míry neefektivní výrobou, těžkým průmyslem a potlačenou individuální bytovou výstavbou a prosazuje se tržní hospodářství. Nastupuje „společnost masové spotřeby," občanská, demokratická společnost, kterou provází nárůst individualismu. V devadesátých létech s „privatizací" - překotnou změnou vlastnických vztahů, se vytváří nová sociologie společnosti, která se promítne do vztahu architekt – klient a vřadí se nový mezičlánek - developer.

Tím chceme říci: do jedinečného segmentu rodinných domů se vepisují a petrifikují „velké i malé" změny ve společnosti, jak seismické sociální změny, které přinesl rok 1989, tak proměny na úrovni potřeb, zájmů a aspirací individua. Právě segment rodinných domů, vil, rezidencí prožívající mimořádný vzestup se stává jedním z nejzřetelnějších ukazatelů toho, kolik sil, talentů bylo v období před rokem 1989 potlačeno a promarněno.

Pro zachycení a deskripci mimořádné dynamiky tohoto segmentu po roce 1989 můžeme použít ty nejobecnější úvahy o dlouhodobém směřování české architektury, tak je vyslovil český kunsthistorik R. Švácha v tezích o „přísnosti" české architektury, vedoucí až do konce devatenáctého století k zakladateli české moderny Jana Kotěrovi.

Při posuzování výstavby rodinných domů můžeme uplatnit regionální hledisko, kdy vedle oblasti Prahy snadno identifikujeme silná regionální centra s významnými tradicemi výstavby rodinných domů, jakými byly a jsou Liberec, Brno, Olomouc, Zlín, Ostravsko a poukázat na realizace v oblastech lázní (vily a rezidence v Karlových Varech, Mariánských Lázních, atd.), Šumavy, Slezka atd. – kde se nachází a vysoce cení zasazení do přírodního kontextu. Neméně zajímavé je vysledování, jak se některá města vyrovnala s překotnými politickými a ekonomickými změnami a začala zhodnocovat svoji tradici jak v občanské, tak následně v kvalitní výstavbě rodinných domů (například Litomyšl, kde řečeno metaforou, „národní obrození ještě neskončilo...", ve které je obsažena hrdost a aspirace města v nových podmínkách po listopadu 1989) a zejména kde se dařilo a daří odolat satelitní výstavbě rodinných domů/sídel v pseudostylu „podnikatelského baroka." V segmentu rodinných domů vyčteme rovněž napětí mezi kulturou a technikou, které na konci pozdní moderny prochází celou architekturou; stavby, které řeší ekologické téma s nejvyšší možnou radikálností (tradiční a přírodní materiály, místní zdroje, obnovitelnost a recyklace, co nejmenší narušení přírody atd.) a na druhém pólu tzv. smart domy. Mezi těmito póly se realizuje celá škála možností a směřování – k nízkoenergetickým domům, k domům cíleně zhodnocujícím zkušenosti akumulované generacemi příslušného regionu, k prostému, zdánlivě jednoduchému stavění, které je výsledkem radikálně promyšleného vzájemně provázaného řešení půdorysu, konstrukce a konceptu provozu domu atd. Neméně zajímavými tématy jsou rozvolnění tradiční typologie rodinného domu (které se promítá do půdorysu, do interiéru i exteriéru), „žánrové stavění", objevení se minimalistických obytných boxů – kontejnerů atd. Rozsah inovativních přístupů z hlediska použitých technologií, naplňování účelu, řešení půdorysu, interiéru a exteriéru, způsobů jakým se respektuje urbánní nebo přírodní kontext je, zdá se, nezměrný. V konečné instanci je za výsledkem, tak jak tomu bylo v celé dosavadní historii, osobnost architekta. Máme v České republice architekty a realizace, které obstojí ve srovnání s mezinárodní scénou?

I v posledních dvou desetiletích se architekti i urbanisté v České republice nadále vyrovnávají se světovými trendy. V porovnání s minulostí, je dnes v době „velmi pozdní moderny", situace daleko komplikovanější a nepřehlednější. Velké ideje a myšlenky moderny – a jejich nepřehlédnutelným a cenným produktem byl i český funkcionalismus - jsou buď realizované, spotřebované, banalizované anebo zprofanované (srvn. paneláková sídliště), vyprázdněné. Navíc obrovské množství informací je dostupné na kliknutí myší u PC, ale o to více postrádáme smysluplný klíč k jejich uchopení. Při navrhování ale vyžadujeme – ještě více grafů, ještě více vizualizací, ještě více zážitků... Do práce architekta nadále a často překvapivě vstupuje „úřad", vlastnosti nových materiálů i možnosti obsažené v tzv. parametrickém navrhování. V neklidné „rozjitřené kultuře" na přelomu XX. a XXI. století narůstá význam jak individuálního bydlení, tak veřejného prostoru. Po rehabilitaci rodinných sídel po roce 1989 přichází na pořad dne rehabilitace veřejného prostoru. Domov, dům, krajina, region se stává místem, kde se odehrává obnova, regenerace, oproštění a uvědomění si podstatných východisek. „Veřejný prostor" jako komunikativní prostor par excellence, se stává místem utváření neformálních, přirozených vztahů a kontaktů. Individuální bydlení vytváří k tomuto „veřejnému prostoru" potřebný smysluplný protipól. Takto lze asi nejlépe rozumět významu individuálního rodinného bydlení – ne ve smyslu předhánění se v náročnosti architektonického a materiálového řešení, ale ve smyslu zakotvení a zhodnocování tradice, vazby na místo, krajinu, region, zemi.

Tato publikace vědomě přináší pozoruhodné realizace, inovativní řešení, která jsou menšinou v záplavě banální produkce. Na fotografiích zachycené a popsané rodinné domy, vily a rezidence tedy nepředstavují mainstream, ale jejich význam je nesporný. Představují realizace, kde se prosadil architekt – vyšel vstříc představám klienta, naplnil nezbytné požadavky, které má splňovat stavba (účelnost, ekonomie provozu, opravitelnost atd.), respektoval kontext místa realizace – výsledkem je kvalitní stavba, která se stala architekturou.

Na 33 představených realizací se můžeme dívat jako svým způsobem klasiku – v těchto rodinných domech se představuje architektura trvalé hodnoty. Položili jsme otázku - máme v České republice architekty a realizace, které obstojí ve srovnání s mezinárodní scénou? Má produkce rodinných domů, vil a rezidencí v České republice vlastnosti, rysy, které zaujmou a přináší i z vnějšího pohledu - z pohledu zahraničního pozorovatele nepřehlédnutelné kvality? Pečlivě provedený reprezentativní výběr staveb a bohatá fotodokumentace vybízí čtenáře k tomu, aby si na tyto otázky odpovídal nejprve sám a aktivně se pokoušel spoluutvářet architektonický diskurs - případně svůj úsudek sdělil autorovi této publikace.

Adam Gebrian

Kvalita české architektury se za posledních 25 let od pádu komunistického režimu neustále zvedá. Pomalu, ale zvedá. Snad nejlépe je to vidět právě na příkladu rodinných domů. Možná proto, že jde o doménu, která vyžaduje nejužší spolupráci, mezi klientem a architektem. Zadavatel je navíc soukromá osoba, která v naprosté většině případů investuje své vlastní peníze a na výsledku, ve kterém hodlá strávit následující roky, mu nesmírně záleží. Výborná architektura tedy nevzniká tak, že klient poskytne architektovi maximální svobodu v tom, ať si dělá, co se mu zachce, jak si ještě stále spousta lidí myslí, ale naopak, většinou z úzkého dialogu mezi klientem a architektem. Vzájemným ovlivňováním, které většinou trvá dost dlouho. Výsledky, které v knize vidíme, jsou závěry dlouholetých procesů. Což mimochodem představuje jednu z brzd většího množství podobných staveb. Pokud chcete něco tzv. nestandardního, spíše než na fakt, že to bude drahé, se musíte připravit na to, že to bude trvat velmi dlouho. V knize najdeme i několik případů, kdy od prvního záměru k realizaci uplynulo více než 5 let a ve výjimečných případech téměř 10 – což pro rodinný dům opravdu není málo. Můžeme si tak prohlédnout výsledky práce velmi trpělivých lidí.

Kenneth Frampton píše v knize *Moderní architektura, kritické dějiny*: ‚Celková architektonická úroveň zemí, které jsou jinak stejně rozvinuté, je však velmi rozdílná; na druhé straně můžeme překvapivě kultivované projevy stavební tvořivosti spatřit v zemích, které bychom jinak považovali za zaostalé.'

Česko (a dříve Československo) nepatří mezi země, jehož architektura by poutala světovou pozornost. Existuje pro to řada důvodů. Jedním z nich je absence osobností-hvězd globálního významu, skrze které by bylo možné přiblížit kvalitu architektury na našem území světu. Nebylo tomu tak v minulosti, není tomu tak teď a pravděpodobně tomu tak ani nebude v blízké budoucnosti. Nemusí to ale být automaticky špatně.

Architekt Ján Stempel vydal v uplynulých letech dvě knihy, které v sobě dohromady slučují 176 individuálně navržených rodinných domů. Tato publikace zahrnuje výběr 33, které i tak ukazují širokou škálu možných přístupů k řešení individuálních potřeb jednotlivých stavebníků. Najdeme tu domy velké, malé (ty převažují), nízké, vysoké, úzké, dlouhé, novostavby, rekonstrukce, na samotě v přírodě, v husté zástavbě centra, na předměstí, na rovině, ve svahu, z betonu, ze dřeva, z cihel, z oceli, moderní, abstraktní, tradiční – se sedlovou střechou, výrazné, nenápadné, introvertní – tedy do sebe uzavřené. Přes rozdílnost odpovědí je možné vystopovat atribut jisté zdrženlivosti, uměřenosti, která jednotlivé stavby spojuje. Je to dáno trochu národní tradicí, a navíc ještě podpořeno osobou architekta, editora, který tak částečně dává najevo svůj žebříček hodnot. V knize tak nenajdeme jedinou stavbu, která by parazitovala na svém okolí a výrazně zhoršovala prostředí pro sousedy, či náhodné kolemjdoucí.

Množství různorodých reakcí na rozdílná prostředí je velmi dobrou zprávou. Jsem dlouhodobě přesvědčen, že úroveň českých architektů je velmi slušná a vychází z kvalit škol, které obstojí v mezinárodním srovnání. Horší je to s celkovou úrovní vkusu společnosti, v demokratických podmínkách, které trvají pouhého čtvrt století. Pohled do nedávné minulosti nám ukazuje, že jsme se výrazně zlepšili v činnostech, které děláme pravidelně. Kupujeme si kvalitnější a nadčasovější oblečení a boty, více se zajímáme o to, co jíme. Se stavěním je to horší, málokdo s ním z pozice zadavatele má opakovanou zkušenost (i když i takové v této knize najdeme). Ne nadarmo jeden z autorů zastoupených v knize, Stanislav Fiala, říká, že nejlepší klient je ten, který už postavil aspoň dva mizerné domy a přesně tak ví, co nechce opakovat.

Množství stavebníků dobrých rodinných domů dává naději, že se po uspokojení svých vlastních soukromých potřeb v oblasti bydlení následně zaměří na zlepšení prostředí, ve kterém pracují, nebo skrze angažmá ve veřejném sektoru dokážou ovlivnit i kvalitu staveb budovaných za veřejné peníze. Ta zatím představuje asi největší problém současné situace v Česku a důvod malé viditelnosti naší architektury na mezinárodní scéně. Nemusí tomu tak ale být navždy.

Mladá Boleslav, Michalovice / Petr Suske (strana 10)

Stoh v krajině – nic nemůže být přirozenější. Ale stoh s deštníkem? Můžeme si ho dovolit, žijeme přece v 21. století. Nosnou kostru tvoří dřevěný obvodový skelet a zděné jádro. Dřevěná konstrukce je obezděna patnácticentimetrovou zdí z nepálených cihel, která vytváří akumulaci a působí příznivě na mikroklima v interiéru. Vnější vrstva tepelné izolace na obvodovém plášti – oddělená od hliněné zdi parozábranou – je vyskládána z balíků slámy, chemicky ošetřených proti hoření. Nad stropní konstrukcí je rozevřený „deštník" z průsvitné folie. Je zavěšený na komínové těleso, které prochází středem domu. Dům je tvořen volným obytným prostorem, organizovaným okolo centrálního, teplého akumulačního jádra, ve kterém jsou umístěny koupelny, zdroj tepla a komín. Na přání klienta je prostorově uzavřena ložnice a hostinský pokoj.

Hráň u Slavonic / Martin Rajniš (strana 14)

Klient zakoupil pozemek v chráněné přírodní rezervaci známé jako Česká Kanada, a to se záměrem postavit mezi loukami a skalami porostlými borovicemi chatku. Nakonec vznikl dům sestávající ze sedmi 3,6m částí, z čehož dvě části na krajích zůstaly otevřené jako terasy. Celá severní stěna je chráněná a tvoří, jako v Japonsku, dlouhý domek s posuvnými dveřmi. Okna na jižní, východní a západní straně jsou osazena zevnitř. Posuvný dilatační kloub umožňuje uchyceným rámům s dvojitým sklem, aby se pohybovaly spolu s vyskládaným dřevem, které mění rozměry v závislosti na změně vlhkosti a na postupném vysychání. Experimentováním s prostorem, tvořeným volně vyskládanými vrstvami dřeva, architekti vytvořili plně obyvatelný dům, v němž tektonika navrstveného dříví poskytuje příjemné a důkladné vnější stínění, které zabraňuje vzniku skleníkového efektu uvnitř budovy.

Brno / Zdeněk Fránek (strana 18)

Nevýhodná poloha budovy, orientované čelem ke strmému severnímu svahu, vedla k návrhu, který domem nechal procházet úzký pruh světla. Obklopující zeleň pak toto světlo ještě filtruje a vylepšuje. Předností tohoto přesného dávkování světla je intenzivní zážitek z výhledu do husté vegetace na Červeném kopci a panoramatický výhled na město. K výstavbě bylo užito kombinace zdění a litého betonu. Kónická část nad garáží tvoří z obou stran přístupný hlavní obytný prostor, bezešvě spojující interiér s exteriérem. Hlavní předností domu je zahrada s meruňkovým sadem, terasou, dvěma betonovými jeskyněmi a akátovou džunglí v horní části pozemku.

Brno – Petr Pelčák (strana 22)

Cílem bylo vytvořit rodinný dům úsporný velikostí a současně velkorysý charakterem obytného prostoru. Prostředkem k tomu byla jednoduchost, proporčnost, provázání stavby s terénem a využití panoramatických výhledů. Vnější rozměr obytného kvádru, umístěného v prudkém jižním svahu, je 7 × 11 m. Tato omítaná obytná část je na skalnatý svah navázána souvisejícími konstrukcemi a plochami z lokálního kamene. Architekturu klasicky stavěného domu s keramickými svislými i vodorovnými konstrukcemi ovlivnila i skutečnost, že je umístěn v nejteplejší lokalitě Brna.

Beroun – HŠH architekti (strana 26)

Na základě abstraktního přemýšlení o prostoru spolu s klientem začal v roce 2001 vznikat dům – Prostorová struktura nebo Prostorová mřížka. Výsledkem je objekt, který představuje výsek z prostorové makrostruktury-sítě o rozměrech 6 × 2 × 2 modulů nebo krychlí (celkový počet modulů je tedy 24). Do této abstraktní struktury je organizován provoz rodinného domu. Každá krychle představuje samostatnou objemovou jednotku, které je podle potřeby určena funkce. Stavba je řešena jako montovaný ocelový skelet s výplněmi z betonu a skla. Jedná se vlastně o stavebnici s nosným modulem krychle o rozměru 3 m. Není zde žádná hlavní fasáda. Není tu žádná hierarchie, všechny části se pojí dohromady stejným systémem. V celém domě jsou eliminovány chodby. Místnosti jsou spojeny různým způsobem a vytvářejí tak prostorovou bohatost stavby, což poskytuje skutečnou flexibilitu užívání.

Semilsko / Rak, Raková, Rydlo, Skalický (strana 30)

Dům je postaven v podhorské oblasti. Měřítko a charakter domu vycházejí z prostředí rozptýlené venkovské zástavby. Vnitřní prostor je spojený s krajinou velkými plochami oken. Součástí domu je krytá veranda s vyhlídkou na hory. Vnitřní prostor domu je otevřený a je vymezen pouze obvodovým pláštěm. Základní prostor tvoří obytný ateliér s galerií v podkroví. Místnosti zázemí jsou sestavené do malého uzavřeného bloku v krajním poli dispozice. Dřevěný přístřešek podél celého domu plní funkci krytého stání pro auto a obytné terasy.

Dům je stavebnice z dřevěného skeletu a obvodového pláště z hliníkových panelů s tepelně izolační výplní. Dřevěná konstrukce je v interiéru pohledově přiznaná. Zvnějšku i zevnitř tvoří povrch stěn a střechy hliníkový plech.

Praha-Liboc / L&P Architektonický ateliér (strana 34)

Pozemek v těsné blízkosti obory Hvězda byl velkou výzvou. Místo, spolu s vlídností majitelů k experimentům architekta, vedlo ke vzniku stavby, která zapadá do rostlé struktury Liboce. Stavba je na severní straně do ulice velmi strohá, do zahrady naopak zcela transparentní. Zasklená štěrbina propojuje dvě části domu – ve větší je hlavní obytná část postavená tak, aby byla podlaha v úrovni zahrady. Pod střechou je umístěn malířský ateliér, lávkou propojený se zahradou. Dispozičně se dům dělí na pánskou část, s hlavním obytným prostorem s kuchyní, kde v zadní části je soukromí pána domu – parní lázeň, whirpool, koupelna, ložnice, pracovna, a část určenou pro paní domu – malířský ateliér, ložnice, koupelna. Obě části jsou propojeny zasklenou lávkou přes štěrbinu mezi dvěma domy. V jižní stěně jsou barevné posuvné desky vytvářející posuvem různá spektra, která mění náladu v interiéru.

Nespeky / Ladislav Lábus AA (strana 38)

Zadáním investorky byla jednopodlažní stavba poměrně malých rozměrů. Dům je navržen s ohledem na optimální využití parcely a stávající zeleně. Architekti jej umístili v poměrně volné, zadní části pozemku, kde vila nejlépe těží z orientace ke světovým stranám, z výhledů na kopce nad řekou i pohledů do vlastní zahrady. Snaha o propojení interiéru s exteriérem a prorůstání domu s okolní rozlehlou zahradou je dovedena do krajnosti: vila je spíše altánem než domem. Hranici mezi vnitřkem a vnějškem potlačují detaily, např. podlahy, nosné stěny, způsob zasklení nebo zastropení stavby i celkový prostorový a hmotový koncept stavby. Atmosféru stavby dotváří jednoduchý design jednotlivých výrobků a prvků i řešení povrchových úprav i volba přírodních materiálů.

Zdiměřice / FIALA+NĚMEC s.r.o. (strana 42)

Dům jako vzpomínka na návštěvu u saharských Berberů. Téměř čtvercový půdorys se zálivem organického tvaru, který nechává vstoupit zahradu dovnitř dispozice. Mnohobarevná kvetoucí zeleň zahrady dotvořila celý pozemek do čistého, uklizeného systému. Divoké stromy zůstaly za plotem – nasvětlené reflektory vytvářejí uklidňující divadlo. Záliv se dá úplně uzavřít posuvnými panely propletenými vrbovým proutím. Vznikla tak venkovní místnost pod dřevěnou pergolou porostlou vistárií. Materiálový i barevný koncept stavby je flexibilní, aby mohl reagovat na požadavky majitelů.
Chloubou domu je jeho technické vybavení. Systém vytápění i chlazení je založen na kombinaci využití tepelného čerpadla a slunečních kolektorů. Využívá se zde stropní a stěnové vytápění, které v létě chladí, a dům tak „dýchá".

Jičín – Roman Koucký architektonická kancelář s. r. o. (strana 46)

Do mírně kosočtvercového tvaru pozemku vložili autoři elipsu vnitřní zahrady, okolo níž se odvíjí vše další. Dům je jednou stranou hradby. Jeho vnější plášť, betonová kvetoucí opěrka, je zároveň severním a západním plotem pozemku. Zbylé části hrany pozemku kryje hradba stromů, celý dům se „obtáčí" kolem zeleného eliptického prostoru. Vnitřní prostory domu postupně od vstupu stoupají. Všechny prostory jsou podél oblé fasády vzájemně propojeny pásem skleněné stěny a dávají tak domu pocit vzájemné sounáležitosti. V náspu mezi domem a opěrnou zdí plotu je ukrytý bazén s malými jiskřičkami stropních světlíků. Malý anglický dvorek vykrojený v náspu za kuchyní dává hlavní obytné místnosti další světlo, vzduch a prostor.

Humpolec – OK PLAN ARCHITECTS (strana 50)

Stavba domu je provedena v blízkosti centra města Humpolce, v mírném svahu, na úzké, podlouhlé parcele o rozloze 430 m2 (včetně domu). Pozemek byl investorovi prodán jako problematicky využitelné plocha. Dům respektuje stávající uliční čáru a reaguje na výškovou úroveň okolní zástavby. Kostru tvoří ocelový, žárově zinkovaný skelet v rastru 6 × 6 × 3 m, přičemž jsou v interiéru veškeré nosné konstrukce přiznané – ocelové nosníky, trapézové plechy, betonové tvárnice, betonové podlahy. Objekt je obložen – potažen cortenovým plechem tl. 4 mm a kopility v 1. NP. Díky své fasádě si získal dům i svou přezdívku, pod kterou je známý veřejnosti, a to – plecháč. Celý interiér je doplněn atypickým nábytkem vyrobeným z MDF desek a opatřený bílou polomatnou barvou.

Květnice / KA architekti (strana 54)

Dům je postaven na pozemku, který kvůli intenzivní výstavbě domů v blízkém okolí trpěl nedostatkem zeleně. Hlavním rysem stavby je dřevěný rám procházející plynule z interiéru do exteriéru, kde tvoří oporu pro popínavé rostliny. Na úrovni střechy tento rám přesahuje přes skleněnou fasádu a sezení pod pergolou, čímž vizuálně spojuje interiér s exteriérem. Vnější struktury vytvářejí jakýsi meziprostor. První patro je cihlové a v interiéru hlavního obytného prostoru je pohledové. Zděná část je zakončena viditelným železobetonovým pohledovým věncem. Zbytek budovy je dřevěný s odhalenou konstrukcí. Štíty a část jižní fasády jsou prosklené, ostatní fasády pak provětrávané a obložené horským modřínem.

Posázaví – sporadical architektonická kancelář (strana 58)

Dům je situován v nejvyšší části severního svahu bývalého arboreta o rozloze 1,57 ha. Přízemí je koncipováno jako jeden prostor se středovým jádrem, do kterého je integrována kuchyňská linka, technická místnost, odkládací prostory, schodiště a krb. Posuvnými stěnami lze obytný prostor s kuchyní oddělit od jižní chodbové části, která je využívána jako zimní zahrada. Jádro umožnilo otevřít obvod panoramatickému výhledu do přírody, která dům těsně obklopuje. Horní patro je tichou a uzavřenou úrovní domu. Ložnice mají úzká okna s průhledy do zahrady. Velké okno nad vanou v koupelně vymezuje pohled do korun strcmů. „Tajné" schodiště vede po fasádě z ložnice na střešní obytnou terasu, která poskytuje místo pro pobyt a odpočinek. Přirozené stínění větvemi vzrostlého dubu a vysoká atika po celém obvodu střechy vytvářejí skryté intimní místo pod otevřenou oblohou.

Zadní Třebaň / Sodomková Sodomka Architekti (strana 62)

Úzký pozemek s nedostatkem slunce v romantickém kraji údolí Berounky, na prudkém lesním svahu, dal vzniknout netradičnímu výškovému členění dvou domů postavených pro dvě sestry: kuchyně s venkovními terasami jsou umístěny v horní úrovni na nejlepším místě pozemku. Jižní okno nad severní částí obytného prostoru přivádí slunce do domu i v prosinci a lednu, kdy je jinak schované za horizontem svahu. Ložnice v nejnižší úrovni zůstávají chladné i v nejparnějším létě. Místo bylo nepřístupné pro techniku, domy jsou proto založeny na mikropilotách vrtaných soupravou odnesenou na zádech. Na ocelových nožkách stojí dřevěná konstrukce domů, která uvnitř, leckde neopláštěna, slouží jako police. Jedlové podlahy, smrkové stěny a modřínová fasáda, ze silných a širokých prken, voní. Velká okna bez rámů umocňují krásu výhledů do údolí.

Brno-Žebětín / Makovský & partners (strana 66)

Domy na mírně svažité parcele nedaleko hřbitova jsou částečně zapuštěny do terénu. Jejich uspořádání reaguje na nepříznivý tvar a orientaci pozemku. Přízemní stavby mají vnější stěny bez oken, všechny obytné prostory v domech jsou kvůli požadavku na odstup od hranic sousedních pozemků prosluněny přes uzavřená atria. Vstupy do domů jsou z mezilehlých atrií na severní straně, klidová zóna s ložnicemi a koupelnou je přístupná z chodby vedoucí podél západní stěny. Obytný prostor s kuchyní se otevírá na jih do atria obehnaného betonovými zdmi. Konstrukce domů je ze směsi litého, tepelně izolačního pohledového betonu. Stěny a strop z tohoto materiálu jsou jednovrstvé, tloušťky 450 a 650?mm. Vnitřní stěny a stěny atrií jsou z klasického pohledového železobetonu, stejně tak i podlahy a betonové prvky v interiéru i exteriéru.

Kojetín / Kamil Mrva Architects (strana 70)

Dům stojí uprostřed obce Kojetín, nedaleko Nového Jičína, na kopci s výhledem. Záměrem investora bylo nejprve zrekonstruovat objekt bývalé stodoly pro bydlení a v budoucnu postavit nový dům v sousedství. Novostavba – ateliér – je vložena do původní stavby, mezi stávající pískovcové zdi a pilíře z roku 1862. Vnitřní dřevostavba se k jihu a k západu otevírá prosklenými stěnami. Koncepce jednoho prostoru vychází z historie bydlení v tomto regionu – vše se odehrávalo v jedné jizbě. V obytném prostoru je kuchyně, jídelna, posezení s pracovnou a ložnice s koupelnou. Terasa má krytou část pro letní posezení a vybíhající sluneční palubu. Nosná konstrukce a lehké zastřešení jsou dřevěné, provětrávaná fasáda je z pohledových cetrisových desek. Prosklené části budovy jsou z izolačního dvojskla s hliníkovými rámy v odstínu fasády.

Kuřim / knesl+kynčl architekti (strana 74)

Jednogenerační rodinný dům se nachází v severovýchodní části města, na úpatí kopce Horka. Třípodlažní cihelný hranol je kolmo vetknut do prudkého svahu s jihovýchodní orientací a výhledem na město. Kompaktní hmota domu je v jednotlivých podlažích vyříznuta tak, aby výsledná forma vytvářela vhodné podmínky pro bydlení z hlediska provozu, osvětlení a orientace ke světovým stranám. V každém podlaží je umístěna jedna samostatná funkční zóna – částečně zapuštěné přízemí obsahuje vstupní prostory, garáž a technické zázemí domu, v prostředním patře se nachází společenská zóna, v nejvyšším podlaží jsou umístěny soukromé místnosti. Všechny obytné místnosti mají přístup na některou z teras a dále do zahrady. Dům je navržen jako zděný, s železobetonovými stropy, obvodová konstrukce je provedena jako sendvičová, s předsazenou stěnou z lícových cihel.

Praha – Šrámková architekti (strana 78)

Dům pro čtyřčlennou rodinu má nepravidelný lichoběžníkový pozemek, který se mírně svažuje k severovýchodu. Jihozápadní část tvoří terénní val vyvýšený o 4 – 6 m nad zbývající část parcely. Val zároveň vytváří přirozené rozhraní s přírodním parkem Drahaň. Jednoduchý kvádr je z části zapuštěný do terénu, z východní strany je k jeho suterénu jako samostatný dilatační celek připojena podzemní garáž. V patře je umístěn otevřený obytný prostor s kuchyní a toaletou. V přízemí je vstup a tři pokoje se společným sociálním zařízením, v suterénu garsoniéra – kancelář, technické prostory a garáž pro dva automobily. K vertikálnímu propojení slouží jednoramenné schodiště u jihovýchodní fasády a výtah v nároží objektu. Dům má monolitickou železobetonovou konstrukci s obvodovým pláštěm z lícových cihel v přírodní barevnosti, opěrné zdi a stěny garáže jsou z pohledového železobetonu.

Brno – Kuba & Pilař architekti (strana 82)

Dům je navržený na půdorysu úzkého obdélníku. Prostorovým základem domu je kvádr, ze kterého jsou „odebírány" jednotlivé hmoty. Největším „odebraným" objemem je vertikální atrium, které rozděluje dům na dvě části. Ostatní „odebrané" hmoty tvoří lodžie a terasy. Orientace obytných místností je na západ do údolí řeky a do atria uprostřed domu. Dům je opláštěný stínícím roštem, který zachovává tvar základního kvádru. V polotransparentním plášti jsou v návaznosti na vnitřní dispozice umístěny otvory, plášť tvoří zábradlí lodžií a vymezuje prostor střešní terasy ve třetím podlaží. Stínící plášť je z černého ocelového pororoštu, černé jsou vnější skleněné obklady lodžií. Většina vnitřních konstrukcí a materiálů je v bílé barvě – sádrové omítky, polyuretanové podlahy, hliníková okna a ocelové schodiště.

Králův Dvůr / OV-A (strana 86)

Pozemek s krásnými výhledy leží v malé, nově zastavované čtvrti na okraji obce. Svažité území stoupá ke kostelu a shora je ohraničeno dlouhou hřbitovní zdí. Zde vznikl dům pro pětičlennou rodinu, postavený důsledně v jedné úrovni, kde mají všichni co nejblíž do obytného prostoru, který stojí v zahradě bez plotu. Přízemní dům na půdorysu čtverce má charakter zahradního pavilonu. Tři soukromé boxy s ložnicemi a zázemím vymezují veřejný prostor, který plynule přechází přes kryté terasy do exteriéru. Namísto plotu na hranici pozemku obepíná fasádu průsvitná šála z modřínových okenic, které kontrolují soukromí interiéru. Po jejich zatažení se terasy stávají dalšími místnostmi v domě. Na základové desce s pasy stojí dřevostavba z I nosníků vyplněná minerální vatou, plochou větranou střechu kryje PVC folie s kačírkem. Prosklené stěny jsou z fasádního hliníkového systému.

Hvozdná u Zlína / Studio Olgoj Chorchoj (strana 90)

Základní objem tvoří dva krystaly, vzájemně pootočené a orientované podle stavebních linií, podpořené jednotným obkladovým materiálem stěn i střechy. Jeden trakt je dvoupodlažní, druhý třípodlažní, čímž je zároveň určeno rozdílné tvarování hmot. Na pozemek se z komunikace nastupuje na úrovni suterénu. Na úrovni obytného patra, tedy druhého podlaží, je dvojice hmot doplněná o bazénovou halu, zapuštěnou do svahu terénu se zatravněnou pochozí střechou. Vzniklé atrium, sevřené trojicí hmot, pootočené na jih směrem k lesu, zaručuje dostatek soukromí a zároveň optické propojení vnitřních prostor. Třetí podlaží, orientované na východ, je ložnicovým patrem rodičů a je odtud možný výstup na střechu bazénu. Nosnou konstrukci objektu tvoří železobetonové monolitické stěny, v místech s otevřenou dispozicí nahrazeny ocelovými sloupy, v části je použitý vodostavební beton.

Pernink / FAM Architekti (strana 94)

Dům stojí v obci Pernink v Karlovarském kraji, v nadmořské výšce 820 m n. m. Dolina podél Hamerské doliny a říčky Bystřice je v mírném spádu a klesá v stejném směru jako převládající větry. V obci je stávající zástavba dvou různých měřítek: malých chalup a větších vícepatrových horských domů. Stavba je kombinací rodinného domu a domu pro hosty s potřebným zázemím pro zimní sporty. Podobu domu formovala topografie terénu a orientace převládajících větrů, proti kterým se dům staví úzkým průčelím. Určující byly také výhledy na protější zalesněné kopce. Konstrukce je ze superizolačního zdiva tloušťky 490 mm. Cesta domem od vstupu směrem do obytné haly v patře prochází dvakrát touto masivní stěnou a vytváří tak pocit intimity a ochrany před vnějším klimatem. Různá hierarchie výšek vnitřních prostor se promítá do hmoty a měřítka stavby.

Buš / Markéta Cajthamlová (strana 98)

Dům se nachází na mírně svažitém pozemku na okraji obce. Stavba ctí propojení s přírodou, okolní zástavba tento hlavní rys domu neruší, pozemek obklopuje vzrostlá zeleň. Dispozice tvoří hlavní obytná místnost s jídelnou a kuchyní, pokoj, dvě ložnice, koupelna se saunou a párou, WC a sklad. Na hlavní obytnou místnost navazuje krytá jižní terasa s vířivkou a přírodní bazének. Nosné zdivo je tvořeno betonovými tvárnicemi suchého zdění, izolované minerální vatou. Fasáda má cedrový obklad na dřevěném roštu. Stropy jsou dřevěné ze sbíjených vazníků, plochá střecha je zelená. Cedr se objevuje i v podhledech i jako materiál okenních výplní. Dům vytápí tepelné čerpadlo vzduch–voda. Systém vytápění je kombinace podlahového topení s radiátory a podlahovými konvektory.

Roudnice nad Labem / Ivan Kroupa (strana 102)

Rodinný dům je začleněný do výběžku nad městem. Betonové zdi, které vyrůstají z terénu, byly ponechány, aby postupně zarostly vegetací a zvolna se staly součástí terénu. Velká skleněná fasáda a terasové křídlo propojují interiér s exteriérem. I uvnitř budova usiluje o splynutí s krajinou: pískový povrch podlah; stropy a zdi splývající s bazénem a vytvářející jakousi krytou pláž s hrubou písčitou úpravou. V obytných prostorách a patrové knihovně jsou povrchy hladce bílé. Pozdější úpravy v zahradě neodpovídají architektonickému návrhu ani nejsou v souladu s rázem podřipské krajiny; nicméně časem by se uměle vytvořené plochy zeleně mohly opět začlenit do svého přirozeného prostředí.

Praha-Lochkov / D3A (strana 106)

Dům je postaven ve starší zástavbě na trojúhelníkovém pozemku s velkým převýšením. Objekt je rozdělen do dvou propojených částí. Při ulici je garáž s krytým prostorem a vstupem s předsíní. Do vnitřního nádvoří se hlavní dvoupodlažní hmota obrací prosklenou fasádou. Dvorek s intimní atmosférou se tak stává součástí velkorysého obytného prostoru spojeného s kuchyní. Pomocné technické provozy jsou zapuštěny do svahu. V patře objektu jsou tři pokoje a chodba se šatnovou stěnou přisvětlená světlíkem. Oba menší pokoje a koupelna mají přístup na terasu. Konstrukce objektu je železobetonová, stejně jako fasády a střecha objektu. Prosklení fasád zakrývají žaluzie a dům vytápí tepelné čerpadlo. Autorem výtvarných objektů je Petr Písařík.k.

Jevany / Architektura (strana 110)

Zděný, přízemní nízkoenergetický dům vyrostl na lesním pozemku naproti rybníku v Jevanech, kde vodní hladina tvoří stále se měnící obraz. Stavba je z jižní strany směrem k rybníku prosklená, jeho zadní strana je zavřená, okna směřují na východ a západ. Půdorysně je členěn na tři výškové úrovně. Zadní trakt tvoří užitkové technické místnosti, v předním traktu jsou obytné místnosti, které jsou všechny situovány k jihu, díky prosklenym plochám však mají navíc i východní nebo západní osvětlení. Dům je příčně rozdělen na tři zóny – pro dospělé, pro děti a společnou obývací. Fasáda je z přírodního kamene, střecha a stropy jsou z pohledového betonu. Podlahy v koupelně jsou lité bílé, stěny jsou obloženy mramorem. Kámen je i v obývacím pokoji, kde tvoří stěnu společně s krbem a kuchyní. Vytápění zajišťuje tepelné čerpadlo, topení je podlahové.

Český ráj / Stempel & Tesar architekti (strana 114)

Rodinný dvojdům byl navržen v II. zóně ochrany přírody a krajiny Chráněné krajinné oblasti Český ráj. Návrh stavby vychází z principu místní lidové architektury, kdy je polovina domu kamenná a polovina dřevěná, čímž byl dům jednoznačně rozdělen na hospodářskou a obytnou část. Dalším inspiračním zdrojem byly průjezdné stodoly, které se v návrhu propsaly do velkých prosklených částí. Tyto průhledy vnáší do interiéru jižní světlo a přitom ponechávají jedinečný severní výhled na les a vrcholky Krkonoš. Vzdušný interiér je v souladu s exteriérem stavby. Hlavním materiálem je dřevo, které je kombinované s barevným vestavěným nábytkem. Jednoduchá forma a přírodní kombinace materiálů dává domu venkovský charakter, aniž by se ztratil současný výraz. I přes poměrně velký objem působí stavba zejména díky materiálovému členění kompaktně.

Vaňov / 3+1 architekti (strana 118)

Stavebníkova vazba k místu a poloha s panoramatickým výhledem do údolí byly klíčovými momenty návrhu domu na jinak ne příliš příznivě orientovaném a strmém pozemku. Dům v mnoha směrech navazuje na původní stavebníkovu chatu (umístění, materiály) a odkazuje také k jejímu tvarosloví (pultová střecha, krytá terasa…). Dům je navržen jako lehký dřevěný skelet založený na betonových pasech spřažených se základovou deskou. Návrh pracuje v horizontálním i vertikálním plánu s modulem 625 mm. S proporcemi pomohl modul dřevostavby a s barevností se autoři inspirovali v přilehlé zahradě.

Stará role / A69 – architekti, s. r. o. (strana 122)

Projekt stoprocentně využívá stavební pozemek. Namísto domu se zahradou architekti stvořili nekonečnou sérii motivů s domem. Budova zabírá celý prostor a smazává přechody mezi vnitřkem a vnějškem a obráceně. Návrh byl primárně založen na typologickém diagramu, který zvažoval požadavky každé místnosti na úroveň soukromí, slunečního světla, kontaktu se sousedy a velikost. Tento diagram měl nakonec tvar spirály. Prostory s většími nároky na soukromí jsou umístěny výše a ke středu parcely. Spirála začíná technickým zázemím blízko vchodu a vrcholí hlavní ložnicí. Povrchy mají jemnou texturu a jsou téměř monochromatické.

Mníšek / KSA (strana 126)

Budova vypadá z ulice jako malý bunkr nebo zemljanka – malá a uzavřená. Vnitřní design nicméně působí zcela opačným dojmem. Šestiúhelníková budova se otevírá k zahradě prostornými skleněnými zdmi s posuvnými dveřmi. Interiér je uzavřený a hlavní roli v něm hrají posuvné příčky a dveře. Strukturu domu tvoří litý beton, nosné zdi pak podpírají strop s klenbou 18 m, který je dále držen vnitřním jádrem, ve kterém jsou umístěny koupelny. Hexagonální betonová skořepinová střecha, terénní vlna a jednoduchá organická forma dovolují plně využít prvky ploché desky. Budova spojuje nejmodernější aktivní i pasivní systémy pro úsporu energie a stabilní vnitřní klima – to podporuje i zatravněná střecha, která přechází v oko ní zahradu.

Zbečno / A.LT architekti (strana 130)

Minimální rodinný dům vznikl na místě nevyhovujícího objektu rekreační chaty z padesátých let. Objekt se nacházel na chráněném území s vyhlášenou stavební uzávěrou. Při navrhování proto přicházela do úvahy pouze „přestavba" stávajícího objektu. Z původního objektu zůstala zachována garáž, která dnes slouží jako technické zázemí. Nový dům stojí, vzhledem k značně svažitému pozemku, na dřevěných sloupech. Půdorys ve tvaru šestihranu lépe reaguje na západní proslunění a výhledy do všech stran. V přízemí je obývací prostor s kuchyní a WC. V patře se nacházejí dva pokoje s pracovnou a koupelnou. Celodřevěná stavba sestává z masivních dřevěných panelů KLH, zvnějšku zateplená a obložená obkladem z nehoblovaného modřínu.

Frýdava / Uhlík architekti (strana 134)

Dům je umístěn ve velké nadmořské výšce (745 m) na strmém svahu u Lipenské nádrže a má nepříznivou severovýchodní orientaci. Návrh se pokouší tyto obtížné podmínky řešit. Dům je rozdělen na dvě části. V níže položené betonové části se nacházejí ložnice, které jsou propojené terasou s okolím, dále je v ní sklep s místností pro wellness a technickým zázemím. Na tomto betonovém základu leží velký kvádr se skleněnou fasádou, který přesahuje na obě strany o 8 m, takže vypadá, jako by levitoval nad stromy u jezera. Otevřený obývací pokoj je plný světla a nabízí panoramatické výhledy na jezero prosklenou fasádou, která může být zacloněna, nebo dokonce úplně uzavřena žaluziemi. Spodní část budovy je tvořena sandwichovými panely ze železobetonu a vrchní kvádr je z vyztužené ocelové konstrukce pokryté ohnivzdornými HPL laminátovými deskami.

Litomyšl – Josef Pleskot (strana 138)

Rodinný dům - umístěný uprostřed pestré stávající zástavby severního okraje města Litomyšl - je na žádost klientů koncipován jako přízemní jednopodlažní „atriový" dům, který je orientovaný do sebe, do centrálního prostoru. Z tohoto nezastřešeného „obývacího pokoje" lze vstoupit do všech ostatních prostor. Vnější fasády přecházejí do ohradních zdí a vytvářejí jakousi tvrdou skořápku - ulitu, která chrání život uvnitř před okolním světem. Směrem dovnitř naopak působí dům měkce a volně prostupně – velké prosklené plochy s množstvím dveří zprostředkovávají propojení vizuální i faktické. Propojení interiéru a exteriéru podporují i venkovní zastřešené terasy obíhající všechny tři vnitřní strany atria. Čtvrtou stranu „obytného dvora" uzavírá vodní plocha a zahrada, jejíž proměny podle ročních období se tak stávají nedílnou součástí života v tomto domě.

Praha / Schindler Seko Architects (strana 142)

Budova je součástí zástavby bývalé obce Tejnka poblíž areálu Pražského hradu. Architektonický návrh obsahoval homogenní třípodlažní novostavbu (včetně nových základů), vloženou do stávajících historických zdí, plus přístavbu a zvýšený půdní obytný prostor. Základní hmotová kompozice má dvě části: obnovenou historickou fasádu a novou přístavbu umístěnou podél jižní strany pozemku.

Objekt přístavby je kompaktní z monolitického pohledového betonu s plochou střechou v úrovni přilehlé ulice a poskytuje místo pro parkování i vstup do domu. Také ve staré budově byly zdi, stropy a schodiště vyrobeny z monolitického betonu, jehož povrch přiznává bednění z přírodních nehoblovaných dřevěných prken. Podlahy jsou pak strojově vyhlazené.